D1521615

Designing Campus Activities to Foster a Sense of Community

Dennis C. Roberts, *Editor*
Lynchburg College

NEW DIRECTIONS FOR STUDENT SERVICES
MARGARET J. BARR, *Editor-in-Chief*
Texas Christian University

M. LEE UPCRAFT, *Associate Editor*
The Pennsylvania State University

Number 48, Winter 1989

Paperback sourcebooks in
The Jossey-Bass Higher Education Series

Jossey-Bass Inc., Publishers
San Francisco • Oxford

Dennis C. Roberts, (ed.).
Designing Campus Activities to Foster a Sense of Community.
New Directions for Student Services, no. 48.
San Francisco: Jossey-Bass, 1989.

New Directions for Student Services
Margaret J. Barr, *Editor-in-Chief;* M. Lee Upcraft, *Associate Editor*

New Directions for Student Services is published quarterly
by Jossey-Bass Inc., Publishers (publication number USPS
449-070). Second-class postage paid at San Francisco, California, and
at additional mailing offices. POSTMASTER: Send address changes
to Jossey-Bass Inc., Publishers, 350 Sansome Street, San Francisco,
California 94104.

Editorial correspondence should be sent to the Editor-in-Chief,
Margaret J. Barr, Sadler Hall, Texas Christian University,
Fort Worth, Texas 76129.

Library of Congress Catalog Card Number LC 85-644751

International Standard Serial Number ISSN 0164-7970

International Standard Book Number ISBN 1-55542-857-6

Cover art by WILLI BAUM

Manufactured in the United States of America. Printed on acid-free paper.

Ordering Information

The paperback sourcebooks listed below are published quarterly and can be ordered either by subscription or single copy.

Subscriptions cost $56.00 per year for institutions, agencies, and libraries. Individuals can subscribe at the special rate of $42.00 per year *if payment is by personal check.* (Note that the full rate of $56.00 applies if payment is by institutional check, even if the subscription is designated for an individual.) Standing orders are accepted.

Single copies are available at $12.95 when payment accompanies order. (California, New Jersey, New York, and Washington, D.C., residents please include appropriate sales tax.) For billed orders, cost per copy is $12.95 plus postage and handling.

Substantial discounts are offered to organizations and individuals wishing to purchase bulk quantities of Jossey-Bass sourcebooks. Please inquire.

Please note that these prices are for the calendar year 1989 and are subject to change without notice. Also, some titles may be out of print and therefore not available for sale.

To ensure correct and prompt delivery, all orders must give either the *name of an individual* or an *official purchase order number.* Please submit your order as follows:

Subscriptions: specify series and year subscription is to begin.
Single Copies: specify sourcebook code (such as, SS1) and first two words of title.

Mail all orders to:
Jossey-Bass Inc., Publishers
350 Sansome Street
San Francisco, California 94104

New Directions for Student Services Series
Margaret J. Barr, *Editor-in-Chief;* M. Lee Upcraft, *Associate Editor*

SS1   *Evaluating Program Effectiveness,* Gary R. Hanson
SS2   *Training Competent Staff,* Ursula Delworth
SS3   *Reducing the Dropout Rate,* Lee Noel
SS4   *Applying New Developmental Findings,* Lee Knefelkamp, Carole Widick, Clyde A. Parker
SS5   *Consulting on Campus,* M. Kathryn Hamilton, Charles J. Meade
SS6   *Utilizing Futures Research,* Frederick R. Brodzinski
SS7   *Establishing Effective Programs,* Margaret J. Barr, Lou Ann Keating
SS8   *Redesigning Campus Environments,* Lois Huebner

Contents

Foreword

Esther Lloyd-Jones

From its inception, the student personnel concept has focused on building a sense of community on the college campus. In 1937 the American Council on Education published *Student Personnel Point of View*. Those of us who drafted the pamphlet set out to define the role of student personnel, which many college educators in the late nineteenth and early twentieth centuries were beginning to find essential. That role would require paying special attention to students and considering them as they lived in community with one another. It has been gratifying to find that the original concepts we sought to define have survived so potently. It should well be so, because the role of the dean of students emerged from and enhanced the total concerns and purposes of the faculty.

This volume, *Designing Campus Activities to Foster a Sense of Community,* is in many ways a revival of the founding precepts of student personnel work. The contributors recognize that while the teaching faculty of a college or university are important, the student personnel can do much to make or break an institution. A college may have a distinguished faculty and—judged separately—a good public relations program, a good admissions and retention strategy, well-planned and -administered residence halls, a large endowment, and so forth. But if the student personnel programs are not also well coordinated, if skillful and understanding attention is not applied to the quality of human relations on the campus, then the students' college experiences will not be as good as they might be, and the college will not affect students' lives as richly and beneficially as it should.

The authors, who have contributed their diverse perspectives to this sourcebook, know that beyond administration there is another important dimension to student personnel work that does not deal exclusively with the individual but that nevertheless enriches campus life. Student personnel experts, besides looking at students as individuals only and serving their individual needs, must see the aggregate of students and the development of relationships, which are the raw stuff of small and, ultimately, large groups. The groups related to one another constitute the community, which thereby becomes a powerful source of energy for the education and development of its members.

Each college or university has its own character, traditions, legends, standards of behavior, and recreational and ceremonial programs. These

1

attributes of student culture give rise to peer groups and the resulting peer shaping and supports. Peer groups are heavily molded by where students live, whether in residence halls or in the broader community off campus. Other opportunities are present as students associate through classes, sports programs, student government, or the pursuit of special hobbies or interests.

The breadth of possibilities for creating a sense of community recalls an original tenet of student personnel work: Student personnel work needed (and now has) a philosophical foundation, a research emphasis, scholarly literature, and professional organizations and publications through which to share their findings. Furthermore, as this volume demonstrates, because student personnel work was never intended to be the province of specific positions or offices, the fulfillment of the mission of student personnel work, namely, the building of community, can only be achieved when student personnel workers share and disseminate their work. The most successful educational and developmental environments will be those that infuse all campus staff with the goals and purposes of student personnel experts.

Many examples can be found to illuminate the importance of community and community building on the campus. The admissions expert must be able to see not only how previous experience and test scores will permit individuals to adjust to the academic environment but how the student community, which results from various mixtures of gender, race, national origin, and other qualities, will prepare these individuals for adult life. As new students acclimate to the campus, they should begin to realize that their new college has a history, legends, and important traditions. The role of older students, faculty, and staff is critical in drawing new students into this understanding. Campus traditions related to values, ethics, and moral exploration are also important in shaping and returning new students into a broad community.

Student personnel programs along with the academic curriculum *are* education. In countless ways they overlap, but each has its own identity. How can faculty teach effectively without being sensitive to their students' needs, feelings, and reactions?

I hope that, with me, you will find *Designing Campus Activities to Foster a Sense of Community* to be both a rediscovery and a new beginning in your understanding of what is possible for us in our roles as student personnel workers. Indeed, we are a community too. As you read and reflect, you will need to define for yourself what community is and what powers lie within this broad concept. The authors themselves will be defining and redefining community throughout these pages.

Before closing, I will venture to provide some notions about community that I find instructive. The condition of community is the binding together of individuals toward a common cause or experience. Individuals both enlarge and restrict their own freedoms by joining such a community. But whatever restriction results is far surpassed by the individual's and the group's ability to achieve established goals while at the same time creating mutual support and pride.

Esther Lloyd-Jones is the author of the landmark text Student Personnel Work *(1929). She served on the faculty of Teachers College, Columbia University, for forty years and has been a national leader in education.*

Student involvement in the life of the college has been found to relate positively to numerous variables, such as satisfaction with college, retention, academic achievement, and loyalty.

Marginality and Mattering: Key Issues in Building Community

Nancy K. Schlossberg

One of the deepest current concerns in higher education is to find ways to more fully involve students in learning. Astin (1977, 1984) found that greater degrees of involvement with the programs and activities of the campus influence student satisfaction with college, academic achievement, and persistence toward graduation. Involvement, "the amount of physical and psychological energy that the student devotes to the academic experience" (1984, p. 297), includes five postulates, two of which are critical in understanding our task of building community on a college or university campus: "The amount of student learning and personal development associated with any educational program is directly proportional to the quality and quantity of student involvement in that program. The effectiveness of any educational policy or practice is directly related to the capacity of that policy or practice to increase student involvement" (p. 298).

Involvement creates connections between students, faculty, and staff that allow individuals to believe in their own personal worth. This involvement also creates an awareness of our mutual relatedness and the fact that the condition of community is not only desirable but essential

D. C. Roberts (ed.). *Designing Campus Activities to Foster a Sense of Community.*
New Directions for Student Services, no. 48. San Francisco: Jossey-Bass, Winter 1989.

to human survival. Therefore, the concern over involving students, although expediently related to satisfaction and retention, is the very process that creates community.

Those working to build a sense of community through activities are challenged to understand why certain individuals get involved, thereby creating community among themselves, and why others seem unable to establish connections or a meaningful level of involvement. The study of patterns of student involvement and what encourages or discourages that involvement could result in more purposefully designed programs and activities that more effectively promote the quality of community. The concepts of *marginality* and *mattering* offer new ways to explore these concerns.

This chapter defines a new construct for specifying how involvement can be achieved. The construct allows us to consider whether students feel marginal or that they matter. Qualities of a mattering environment will be described and the issue of *rituals*, which provide a sense of mattering, will then be explored.

Marginality Versus Mattering

We are aware of classifications and issues that divide us. There are many—ethnicity, age, gender, social class, sexual preferences, religion, and politics, to name a few. This awareness of different experiences, different expectations, and different voices raises a perplexing set of questions: With all these differences separating us, what connects us? Do we have a shared humanity? Can a campus community be created that allows all students to find a place of involvement and importance?

The polar themes of marginality and mattering connect all of us—rich and poor, young and old, male and female. Are we part of things; do we belong; are we central or marginal? Do we make a difference; do others care about us and make us feel we matter? I will now examine these two constructs, marginality and mattering, and illustrate how students deal with these issues through the college experience, how differently they work with them depending on their age, gender, social class, ethnic and religious identifications, and the state of their emotional and financial resources. These two issues, which illustrate continuity and change in life, have been relatively unexamined. They may have great significance.

My work on transitions—events or nonevents that alter our lives—convinced me that people in transition often feel marginal and that they do not matter. Whether we are entering first grade or college, getting married, or retiring, we are concerned about our new roles. We wonder, will we belong? Will we matter? Although this is not the case for everyone, its recurrence in my interviews of people in transition led me to a search that is still in progress—a search for a clearer understanding of the human condition.

Marginality. At work, where I have been a professor for twelve years, I feel central, important. I belong. However, when I walk into a student dining area or when I visit my son's school for parents' night, I feel marginal. For some reason, it seems that people don't smile at or talk to me. Why do I feel marginal in one place and central in another? Perhaps some of the answer lies in the different approaches that exist for understanding marginality.

Instances of feeling marginal are numerous. Young people report feeling "out of things" when they enter junior or senior high school or, especially, when they go off to college. People moving from one city to another often feel marginal. We are often nagged by the question, do I belong in this new place?

Every time an individual changes roles or experiences a transition, the potential for feeling marginal arises. The larger the difference between the former role and the new role the more marginal the person may feel, especially if there are no norms for the new roles. The first students of nontraditional age to attend traditional campuses, for example, faced such problems. They had no norms to anticipate their pioneering role.

Marginality has also been applied to describe a personality type. Robert E. Park labeled the marginal person as "one who is living and sharing intimately in the cultural life and traditions of two distinct peoples, never quite willing to break, even if permitted to do so, with past and traditions, and not quite accepted, because of prejudice, in the new society in which the individual seeks to find a place" (Park, 1928, p. 892). In describing what happens psychologically to this marginal person, Stonequist postulates that the person experiences "pride and shame, love and hate, and other contradictory sentiments . . . such individuals are constantly aware of their status and turn their attention upon themselves to an excessive degree: thus increased sensitiveness, self-consciousness, an indefinable malaise, inferiority and various compensatory mechanisms, are common traits" (Stonequist, 1935, p. 16). In some cases, individuals become "obsessed" with the problem of marginality, and this becomes their dominant mode of thinking and behaving. They often become professionally involved in the topic of their marginality. For example, some who are learning disabled spend their lives studying learning disabilities or running support groups for students who have special needs.

Marginality can also refer to a permanent condition. For many bicultural individuals, marginality is a way of life. In contrast with the person who moves to a new city or new job, a bicultural person feels permanently locked between two worlds. This individual identifies with two cultures simultaneously. International students in the United States try to relate well to American culture but are still proud of their national origins. A Hispanic student from this country feels American but also takes pride in being of Spanish descent. Each culture defines its marginal groups and designates certain groups as invisible or invalid. Ralph Ellison's landmark book *The Invisible Man* (1972) dealt with the invisibility of blacks. More recently Evelyn Torton Beck (1982) has referred to the invisibility of gays and lesbians. However, people within a culturally defined marginal group may not suffer from marginality when they are centrally involved in that group.

Apparently marginality can be a temporary condition during transition, a description of a personality type, or a way of life. Clearly this is a complex, almost overwhelming subject, which could leave student affairs staff and counselors perplexed about what, if anything, to do. However, they could begin by dividing the situations into those that are transitional and those that seem permanent. Social action can alleviate permanent marginal status; therapy can relieve an obsession with marginality. For individuals in transition from one role to another or for groups in transition, like new students, the development of rituals can be useful and innovative. (Rituals are discussed later in this chapter, and a specific example of a new student transition ritual is explained in the Appendix.)

We can conclude that everyone is marginal from time to time. The college freshman, marginal at first, can become a part of the community, yet this same person will feel marginal many more times in life—possibly after graduation on entering the job market or moving to a new city. This issue affects everyone differently. Often, feeling marginal leads us to conclude that we do not matter or confuses us about the group to which we do. Joining a campus student organization can evoke feelings of marginality. It can take time for students to feel central to a group, as if they matter to others. In short, marginality elicits feelings about mattering.

Mattering. The sociologist Morris Rosenberg and his colleagues suggest that "mattering is a motive: the feeling that others depend on us, are interested in us, are concerned with our fate, or experience us as an ego-extension exercises a powerful influence on our actions" (Rosenberg and McCullough, 1981, p. 165). Their research shows that adolescents who feel they matter, regardless of their self-concepts, will be less likely to commit delinquent acts. Although their research focused on adolescents, they suggest that "one problem of retirement is that one no longer matters; others no longer depend on us" (p. 179). This suggests an interesting question for further study: Do those retirees who feel they matter to others in their new roles adjust more easily to retirement than those who feel they do not? I remember hearing Lee Bradford (founder of National Training Laboratory) describe his shock after retirement when his phone no longer rang. He was not the "elder sought-after statesman." In fact, he realized that his former colleagues felt obliged to have lunch with him when he was in town. Contrast that with the words of an eighty-three-year-old man who feels he matters: He is on the board of a hospital and is currently raising money for a center for abused children. He describes having time to go out each night but time for golf only once a week. "I must say that a lot of people think I am silly at my age to be doing all these things, yet I see so many of my friends who have nothing to do. I feel the hospital needs me, and my special friend needs me." Consider, too, the quandary of students whose lives were the center of their families' attention and who then go off to college, only to find that the family can survive very well without them. What about the high school football hero who is just one of many on a college campus?

Mattering is paradoxical. That both adolescents and older persons need to feel they matter is axiomatic. However, in early and mid life, the relationship between mattering and *satisfaction* might be quite different. In contrast with the earlier example of the student whose absence is not felt is the likelihood that the more one matters—to doting parents, for example—the more pressured, more stressed, and less satisfied one becomes. The research on mid-life women presents another example. Women often consider themselves the "kin-keepers." They care for the various generations and keep in touch on family matters. They are the "ministers of the interior," while men serve as connections to the outside world (Hagestad, 1985). When, then, is mattering essential to well-being and when does it become a burden? The search for an answer has led to several efforts to develop an index for measuring the degree to which people feel they matter (Schlossberg, LaSalle, and Golec, in press; Morris Rosenberg, personal communication, June 1985).

This approach requires a clear definition of mattering. Rosenberg states that mattering is the "direct reciprocal of significance." "Significant others" refers to those we count as significant. Mattering refers to our belief, whether right or wrong, that we matter to someone else. This belief acts as a motivator. Students may not attend a school far from home because it would require leaving friends or parents, who depend on them. Adolescents and young adults with depression may rule out suicide if they feel they matter to others.

Using this construct, we conducted structured interviews with twenty-four men and women ranging in age from sixteen to eighty. These interviews took four aspects of mattering identified by Rosenberg—attention, importance, ego-extension, dependence—and looked at the degree to which the interviewees experienced mattering in three domains of life, namely, close interpersonal relationships, work, and voluntary/community activities. These interviews led to the addition of another dimension—appreciation—to the construct of mattering (see below).

Attention. "The most elementary form of mattering is the feeling that one commands the interest or notice of another person" (Rosenberg and

McCullough, 1981, p. 164). Think for a moment how lonely it feels when we go to a new city, new job, or new setting, where we know no one and where no one would notice if we did not appear. A woman who had a sick, demanding husband and two demanding teenagers always felt "at the end of her rope." When her husband died and, soon after, her children went away to school, she was disconcerted that no one noticed or cared when or if she came home.

Importance. "To believe that the other person cares about what we want, think, and do, or is concerned with our fate, is to matter. Whether the adolescent goes on to college or becomes hooked on drugs may deeply concern his/her parents" (Rosenberg and McCullough, 1981, p. 164). Mattering does not necessarily mean approval. How often do we hear young people say to their parents, "Stop bugging me"? The young person knows, however, that the bugging indicates caring if not approval.

Ego-Extension. Ego-extension refers to the feeling that other people will be proud of our accomplishments or saddened by our failures. In other words, we feel that our success will be the success of another and our failure, the other's failure. Although knowing that our failures are critical to another can be a burden, it also reconfirms that we matter to someone.

Dependence. Rosenberg and McCullough (1981) write: "That our behavior is influenced by our dependence on other people is easily understood. . . . What is . . . more mysterious is why our actions are equally governed by their dependence on us" (p. 165). We all know how it feels to depend on someone else; we also know how it feels to have others depend on us. A college sophomore, deeply depressed and possibly suicidal, was unable to complete a course of study or prepare for a career but got out of bed each day to be at play rehearsals because "they need me." Being needed saved a life.

There is, however, a dark side of dependence. One of the interviewees in our study, a woman in mid life, reported that she gave up graduate work and changed her work hours because of her mother-in-law's and her mother's illness. Despite her constant attention, her mother became difficult, refusing to eat and at times hitting her. This, coupled with her eleven-year-old daughter's depression, was almost too much to bear. The woman mattered too much. As the interviewer, Karen Swetz, wrote: "This is an actual case of a 'sandwich generation' couple. They are being pulled from both sides. They are depended upon by their parents . . . by their siblings . . . by their children . . . and also by their employees. They perceive they matter too much" (Schlossberg, LaSalle, and Golec, in press).

Appreciation. In our interviews we identified another aspect of mattering, appreciation. Over and over our interviewees expressed the importance of feeling that their efforts were appreciated. One person mentioned that the boss only noticed what was done wrong and never mentioned the positive contributions. The woman in the sandwich generation felt clearly unappreciated by her mother, who hit her. How many times have parents needing care been less appreciative of the daily care giver than of the son or daughter who lives far away and calls once a month? And how often do we make extra efforts at work when we feel appreciated?

To design a scale for measuring the degree to which people feel they matter, we generated items based on the interviews. We included items for each domain so that we could differentiate feelings of mattering at home, at work, and in the community. To look at mattering as neither good nor bad, we designed a five-point Likert scale on which respondents mark the degree to which they feel they matter. Respondents were asked to indicate when mattering is beneficial and when it is counterproductive. As one woman said, "I dread the prospect of moving from a period of being stretched beyond my capacity to anticipating not being needed" (Schlossberg, LaSalle, and Golec, in press).

We are now examining institutions and the degree to which they make their constituents feel they matter. Recently we studied adult learners who had participated in some of the nontraditional educational options designed and promoted by the Council for the Advancement of Experiential Learning (Schlossberg and Warren, 1985). Many adult learners felt they mattered to an adviser or to an institution. This feeling kept them engaged in their learning. We realized that a mattering scale could be used by institutions of higher education (Schlossberg, LaSalle, and Golec, in press). This scale, currently being validated, should enable institutions to answer these questions: Do they make students feel they matter? Are their policies, practices, and classroom and cocurricular activities geared to making people feel they matter?

In summary, mattering refers to the feeling that you matter to another; significance refers to those people who matter to you. If what Rosenberg suggests and what we are exploring is true—that mattering is a motive and does determine behavior—we need to make sure our programs, practices, and policies are helping people feel they matter. When a traditional Freudian therapist went to her patient's high school graduation, it enabled the patient to feel she mattered. When institutions of higher education devote desk space to the concerns of adult learners and provide relevant secretarial and message services and activities, adult learners can feel they matter. When an activity program is designed to reach all learners, it can help all students feel connected and involved.

We will discover that mattering is important all through life—people need to feel that they count, they belong, they matter. When this is so, they no longer feel marginal. We will also discover that mattering is played out differently depending on one's transitions, sex, and social class.

By examining mattering across spheres of life, we can get a more complete picture of the individual. People may feel they matter too much at home and not enough at work. This information provides some guidelines for intervention. But describing marginality and mattering is not enough. There is a critical need to help people deal with marginality so that they will eventually matter. Rituals can help. They sometimes occur naturally, but if they do not, then inattention to ritualistic passage can result in the individual feeling isolated. The next section describes the affirmation of rituals.

Rituals

The film *Rites of Renewal* shows the late anthropologist Barbara Myeroff discussing the role of rituals, ceremonies, or rites of passage in helping people deal with marginality by marking "the transition of an individual from one phase of life . . . to another" (Myeroff, 1985). Rituals help people make sense out of the contradiction and paradox of many transitions—the paradox being that there is no single truth, there are many truths; that individuals are part of the past, but also the future.

In this film Myeroff describes the three stages of a ritual. First, the individual is segregated. Look at any ceremony—graduation, retirement, wedding—to observe the separation made obvious by placement or dress of the persons in question. Second, the individual moves into a feeling of being between the old role and the new role—what Victor Turner (1977) labels *liminality*. The person is still a baby and not a baby; still a worker, not a worker. As Myeroff states in the film, "That middle stage, the marginal one, the liminal one, is an especially interesting one because that's where the person is neither one thing or another." Although most people pass through this stage, Turner explores "how whole sets of people can be marginal like tricksters, clowns, poets, medmen"—people who do not fit into any category. The final phase of the ritual is "rein-corporating the person . . . back into society as a new creature with a new identity" (Myeroff, 1985). For example, high school graduates enter-ing college are not sure of their identities. The final phase of the transi-tion will be when they develop identities other than those connected to the high school roles and relationships they previously had.

Ceremonies help define the person; they segregate or single out a person in the company of a meaningful community or group. A personal example might illustrate this point. One night our daughter announced that she was not going to college, that she had a job and planned to move into her own apartment. We were startled. Coincidentally, I attended a lecture by Myeroff in which she discussed the importance of rituals in helping people deal with marginal periods; that is, when they are moving from one phase of life to another. Our eighteen year old was doing just that; she was moving from adolescence to adulthood. We took Myeroff's lecture to heart and decided to ritualize Karen's departure by giving her a celebration dinner and inviting some close family friends. Everyone chose gifts, wrote poems to commemorate her past, and presented them at the dinner table. Our gift was the promise to pay for the installation of a telephone (connecting her to her past) while reminding her that she would pay the monthly charges (propelling her to adulthood). This helped our daughter cope with a transition in which she did not feel like a child anymore yet was not quite grown up. It also helped us define this as a positive, not a negative, transition.

The problem is that for many transitions we have no rituals. We ritualize the entry to and final departure from the college environment, but for many other transitions—completing a project or program for a student organization, selecting a major, separating from a relationship— we have no rituals. How would we ritualize and dignify an adult's return to college when most students are of traditional college age? How could the decision of a student to "stop out" or transfer be acknowledged and affirmed as a legitimate decision? These students are in a liminal, marginal state with no rituals to help them deal with the separation. Because individuals in transition often feel isolated and vulnerable, ceremonies connecting them to society or to the group keep them from feeling lost.

Many life changes have no rituals. Myeroff (1985) devoted a great deal of energy to teaching people how to develop rituals for themselves at these lost moments, to "punctuate and clarify that otherwise amorphous condition." In the film *Rites of Renewal,* a divorce ritual is shown. A minister calls together the divorcing parents and has them repeat an oath of caring but unconnecting. He then addresses the children and has the parents pledge their care, concern, and love for them even though their love for each other has vanished. In-laws and friends now enter the ceremony. Many who watch the film cry during this sequence, probably because we have all been intimately connected with dissolutions that have not had the aid of community and definition. Ritual, though not a panacea, can help people with lifelong issues of marginality and mattering.

Conclusion

Marginality and mattering are two issues that have not been elaborated in psychological and student development literature. Marginality is at one pole, mattering at the other. Identification of these issues adds understanding to some of our complex feelings and can help us develop new coping strategies.

Furthermore, by looking throughout the campus at the diverse backgrounds and experiences of students, we can begin to understand what continues and what changes during the college experience. There will be many continuous aspects that enable students to recognize themselves as they move to new living environments, change academic majors, and take on new leadership roles; there will also be many discontinuous aspects of their college lives. This approach makes it possible to communicate with all students; for whether they are traditional or nontraditional, gifted or average, male or female, all students are concerned about belonging and mattering. As people tell us their stories, we can listen in ways that connect us. As we listen to students and plan activities with them, we need to hear the common underlying concerns: will they fit in, will they matter? Despite these commonalities, we must acknowledge individuality. However, the most important lesson is that even with our differences, we are connected by the need to matter and the need to belong.

The creation of environments that clearly indicate to all students that they matter will urge them to greater involvement. Such involvement should lead to the accomplishment of the goals with which Astin (1977, 1984) has challenged higher education. Clearly, institutions that focus on mattering and greater student involvement will be more successful in creating campuses where students are motivated to learn, where their retention is high, and ultimately, where their institutional loyalty for the short- and long-term future is ensured (Schlossberg, Lynch, and Chickering, 1989).

As you continue reading this volume, consider these questions:

- Do institutional policies assure all students that they matter, that their presence is valued?
- Do programs and services encourage involvement in all aspects of the institution and indicate that each student is unique and important to the institution?
- What new initiatives could be undertaken to draw the marginal student more into campus life?
- How can the campus community itself be encouraged to think of issues of marginality and mattering?
- What are some key characteristics of an educational community that make mattering a high priority for all its community members?

References

Astin, A. W. *Four Critical Years: Effects of College on Beliefs, Attitudes, and Knowledge.* San Francisco: Jossey-Bass, 1977.
Astin, A. W. "Student Involvement: A Developmental Theory for Higher Education." *Journal of College Student Personnel,* 1984, 24, 297–308.
Beck, E. T. *Nice Jewish Girls: A Lesbian Anthology.* Trumansburgh, N.Y.: Crossing Press, 1982.

Ellison, R. *The Invisible Man.* New York: Vintage Books, 1972.

Hagestad, G. "Vertical Bonds: Intergenerational Relationships." In *The Adult Years in Videorecording: Continuity and Change.* Alexandria, Va.: American Association for Counseling and Development, 1985.

Myeroff, B. "Rites of Renewal." In a film produced by N. K. Schlossberg and others, *The Adult Years: Continuity and Change.* Owings Mills, Md.: International University Consortium, 1985.

Park, R. E. "Hunan Migration and the Marginal Man." *American Journal of Sociology,* 1928, *33,* 892.

Rosenberg, M., and McCullough, B. C. "Mattering: Inferred Significance to Parents and Mental Health Among Adolescents." In R. Simmons (ed.), *Research in Community and Mental Health.* Vol. 2. Greenwich, Conn.: JAI Press, 1981.

Schlossberg, N. K., LaSalle, A., and Golec, R. *Mattering Scale.* College Park: University of Maryland, in press.

Schlossberg, N. K., Lynch, A. Q., and Chickering, A. W. *Improving Higher Education Environments for Adults: Responsive Programs and Services from Entry to Departure.* San Francisco: Jossey-Bass, 1989.

Schlossberg, N. K., and Warren, B. *Growing Up Adult.* Columbia, Md.: Council for the Advancement of Experiential Learning, 1985.

Stonequist, E. V. "The Problem of the Marginal Man." *American Journal of Sociology,* 1935, *41,* 3-16.

Turner, V. W. *The Ritual Process Structure and Antistructure.* Ithaca, N.Y.: Cornell University Press, 1977.

Nancy K. Schlossberg is professor of counseling and personnel services, University of Maryland, College Park. She is a recognized proponent of concern and attention for adult students.

There is a growing awareness that student development efforts must focus on the campus environment as well as on individual students.

Understanding the Campus Community: An Ecological Paradigm

Gerardo M. Gonzalez

An appropriate way for a campus activities worker to prepare for the task of assessment is to look at the desired outcome. The proposition of this volume is that one important outcome is the creation of a community that establishes a sense of mattering for its members. Many texts in student affairs and higher education leave the chapter addressing assessment until the conclusion. This sourcebook, however, presents environmental issues and their relationship to assessment early in the text because assessment must be considered throughout activities program planning and is actually an interactive dimension of the overall program initiative.

As indicated throughout this volume, building a sense of community is basic to student affairs work. Since the publication of *Student Personnel Point of View* (American Council on Education, 1937), student personnel have been encouraged to pay attention to the campus environment. This focus contributed to the acceptance of the concept of *in loco parentis* as an early foundation for the student personnel profession. However, in loco parentis primarily served as a legal directive and therefore lacked the depth in theoretical and conceptual roots to make it relevant in today's

D. C. Roberts (ed.). *Designing Campus Activities to Foster a Sense of Community.*
New Directions for Student Services, no. 48. San Francisco: Jossey-Bass, Winter 1989.

environment (Hurst, 1987). In its place, during the 1960s, student development emerged as the conceptual foundation of student affairs programs. Unfortunately, student development theories have perhaps not given enough emphasis to the environment. Because these theories emerged from developmental psychology, they focused almost exclusively on the individual. Thus, even though in their review of student development theories Widick, Knefelkamp, and Parker (1980) noted that development is a product of the interaction between person and environment, Rodgers (1980) rated only four of twenty-four developmental theorists as placing a high emphasis on environment. Campus ecology theory (Banning and Kaiser, 1974) has reminded us of the importance of broadening student development theories to more fully include environmental issues. These issues can then be related to Schlossberg's qualities of mattering (see Chapter One) to assist us in designing programs and environments of highest quality for students.

Central to the concept of campus ecology is the notion of environmental assessment and design (Conyne and Clack, 1981; Huebner, 1979). The purpose of this chapter is to illustrate the application of an ecological paradigm to campus activities programs. The functions of campus activities staff, who act as ecological consultants to the campus community, will be highlighted.

The Ecological Consultant

The roles and functions proposed here for the campus activities worker represent a direct application of the ecological paradigm developed by Trickett, Kelly, and Vincent (1985) for community psychology research. This chapter extensively paraphrases the original writing but places it in the context of the ecologically minded campus activities worker. According to the authors, "To think ecologically is to consider how persons, settings, and events can become resources for the positive development of communities; to consider how the resources can be managed and conserved; and to approach research so that the effort expended will be helpful to the preservation and enhancement of community resources" (p. 285).

The ecological paradigm is based on four biological principles: resource cycling, interdependence, adaptation, and succession. These principles provide useful guides for prevention and developmental programs designed to support adaptation to the life of a particular community (Mann, 1987). The four ecological principles were expanded into ten specific principles for guiding community research and intervention (Trickett, Kelly, and Vincent, 1985). Figure 1 lists these ten principles, and the following discussion represents an application of each principle to campus activities programs.

Figure 1. Ten Principles Embodying the Spirit of Ecological Inquiry

Cycling of Resources
1. Persons, settings, and events are resources for the development of the community and the research relationship.
2. The ecological paradigm advocates the conservation, management, and creation of resources.
3. The activating qualities of persons, settings, and events are emphasized.

Adaptation
4. Coping and adaptation are the dominant means of growth and change.
5. The search for systematic events illuminates the process of adaptation.

Interdependence
6. Persons and settings are in dynamic interaction.

Succession
7. Persons, settings, and events are assessed over time.

Research Relationship
8. Community research and the research relationship are designed to be coupled with the host environment.
9. Attending to the side effects of community research is a priority.
10. Ecological inquiry is a flexible, improvisational process.

Source: Trickett, Kelly, and Vincent, 1985.

Persons, Settings, and Events. The campus activities worker, acting as community consultant, must be able to understand and relate to the local institutional and community culture. This process requires the identification of persons, settings, and events that may serve as community resources. Persons considered resources include those in a position of influence, those who enjoy status within their own groups, and those who themselves have access to diverse and multiple resources (Trickett, Kelly, and Vincent, 1985). On a college campus, these might include the dean of student affairs, program directors, mental health counselors, resident assistants, student activities planners, social chairpersons for Greek fraternities, interested faculty, editors and writers of student and university publications, and student leaders. A central assessment task of the campus activities staff is the identification of these resource persons, whoever they may be on a particular campus. Their mobilization and leadership in involving students is crucial to long-term success. Settings represent those structural elements of the environment that mediate interventions; they include both physical context (for example, a residence hall) and social organizations (for example, the interfraternity council). The campus activities staff should identify the settings where institutional norms and values manifest themselves and are validated. Settings should blend everyday campus life with events and topics related to student development. In addition to existing settings, staff should consider potential settings, whose absence may be discouraging student involvement. For example, the creation of a center to coordinate student participation in volunteer service might increase the opportunity for student involvement. The presence of a volunteer center also clearly indicates what matters to the institution—service to others, altruism, and students who give life to those values.

Events are resources in that they are examples of the norms, processes, and values in the community (Trickett, Kelly, and Vincent, 1985). Schlossberg's emphasis on rituals is particularly relevant here (see Chapter One); key annual events are rituals that help to define the importance of individuals. Events can also create opportunities for interchange between the activities program staff and persons in the setting. Campus activities staff can be known as persons rather than employees of an institution.

Events can be planned or unplanned. An example of an unplanned event might be an alcohol-related traffic accident in which students are injured. Both types of events provide the staff with opportunities to discuss situations and how to respond to them.

It is important that persons, settings, and events be seen as interacting resources (Trickett, Kelly, and Vincent, 1985). The specific persons involved in the activities program naturally affect the settings and events where these persons interact.

Conservation, Management, and Creation of Resources. A fundamental criterion for developing an activities program is the program's impact on the resources the campus requires for its current needs and its future development. There are many programs that compete with student activities for available resources. Therefore, the campus activities staff must give priority to the conservation of resources. A realistic assessment of available resources and how they can be conserved is an important first step. Second, the management of resources requires painstaking formulation of overall plans and procedures. Finally, the creation of resources requires anticipating problems and developing mechanisms to direct the future of the program and ensure that resources are allocated for these long-range plans. An example of considerable complexity would be the creation of a comprehensive curricular and cocurricular leadership program (Roberts, 1980), which requires careful planning, resource identification, and phasing in over a long period. Lasting change does not come quickly.

The Activating Qualities of Resources. This principle emphasizes the proactive rather than reactive nature of the first principle, which stresses treating persons, settings, and events as resources. The campus activities worker should understand how events already available or that occur as part of the natural environment impact student development. What campus events focus on student involvement in learning? What programs and policies demonstrate the priority given to providing services to students? In what settings are such events likely to occur? Who on campus consistently leads and guides such efforts?

Applying the ecological paradigm, the ability of campus activities staff to become a meaningful resource depends on the extent to which they identify and understand such activating behavior, the people involved, and the context within which they function. A contemporary program and counseling issue for many student affairs staffs is acquaintance rape. As an active resource, the student culture can be activated to begin a dialogue on this and other issues. Pronouncements and policies do little until the relationship between student values and behaviors is appreciated.

Coping and Adaptation. Growth and change occur in a community by means of coping and adaptation. Coping refers to the efforts of individuals and settings to deal competently with crisis and stress. Adaptation includes policies and beliefs that individuals and settings have developed over time to maintain themselves and the integrity of their activities (Trickett, Kelly, and Vincent, 1985). A focus on coping and adaptation encourages the campus activities planner to look at how the setting has traditionally coped with and adapted to student development efforts; how the notion of student development is defined by the local campus culture; and how the effort to build acceptance for the campus activities program is managed.

A frequent complaint on many campuses is that "apathy is rife here." The activities planner is, obviously, attempting to reverse this reality or perception, whichever it is. As initiatives are taken to provide new activities in these settings, the planner may confront a long-standing coping behavior that perpetuates the perception of apathy: Students may deliberately not express commitment and enthusiasm for these new activities. With each initiative, the activities planner must understand this dynamic. Placing students in charge of planning is a critical resource in overcoming this debilitating coping response.

Campus activities staff should be aware, for example, that the use of psychoactive substances, particularly alcohol, is closely related to cultural norms and peer group expectations (Berkowitz and Perkins, 1985). Additionally, some evidence suggests that efforts to reduce alcohol use by raising the legal drinking age can result in more surreptitious drinking without a decrease in consumption among college students (Hughes and Dodder, 1986). If students perceive alcohol and drug education programs, like drinking-age laws, to be antithetical to the established culture, their efforts to cope with and adapt to the resulting stress will likely lead to undesirable behavior patterns. Therefore, the campus activities staff must be prepared to revise procedures and program formats to achieve a sense of mutual ownership between themselves and students. Moreover, because of the gradualness of cultural change, coping and adaptation should not be judged solely on the basis of the immediate success of a particular intervention. Evaluation should also consider the preparatory value of the program for future change in the culture (Trickett, Kelly, and Vincent, 1985).

Systemic Events and Adaptation. Systemic events are those that can have positive or negative effects on both individuals and groups on campus. Systemic events, such as the implementation of a new policy on alcohol and drugs, the capture of an athletic championship, or the appointment of a key administrative official, can carry campus-wide implications. They can mobilize individuals in certain campus activities or cause organized groups to take action for a common cause (Trickett, Kelly, and Vincent, 1985). Applying the mattering concept can accentuate a systemic event—for example, making sure that when student elections occur the transition is marked by a significant campus observance, such as swearing in the elected persons or passing the gavel. Such observances recognize the importance of the individuals involved, thus underscoring a sense that they matter.

Because of their power to mobilize the community, ritualistic systemic events can highlight the deeply held norms, values, and adaptation patterns prevalent on a particular campus. These norms and values are likely to provide important information about how people fit, or matter, on their campus. As campus activities staff gain an understanding of systemic events, they can use the knowledge of the events' effects on the community to mobilize resources of the activities program. To accomplish this objective, however, the staff must actively participate in campus events. Appointment to powerful committees, media event planning boards, and other resources that define ritual events should be a priority for these professionals.

Interdependence. The variability or consistency in a person's behavior from one setting to another is the focus of this principle. Students respond according to their defined role in the activity. For example, a fraternity leader may behave very differently at a social event sponsored by an alcohol awareness committee for Greek leaders than at a spring break party sponsored by his own fraternity. Through understanding the behavior expressed by the same individual in contrasting settings, the campus activities worker can develop strategies that allow students to contribute to their environments. The same fraternity leader can be encouraged not only to speak eloquently about the need for Greek involvement in alcohol education but also to assure that his own fraternity follows the responsible-hosting guidelines promoted through the program. By paying careful attention to the dynamic interaction of persons and settings within the campus community, the campus activities staff attempt to minimize the risk of influential persons giving contradictory messages in different settings.

Succession. Communities exist in a state of dynamic equilibrium. Depending on the balance of critical forces, communities can exhibit resistance or receptivity to change (Trickett, Kelly, and Vincent, 1985). A longitudinal time perspective allows the campus activities staff to determine when the campus community is in an accepting phase of change. At such time, the campus might manifest a ready interest in new campus activities. The determination requires campus activities staff to learn about the historical forces that have shaped the campus community. This can be accomplished by talking with persons who have been at the institution for a long time, learning about memorable rituals, studying archival data, and exploring with key campus informants how current norms and policies have evolved.

It is unrealistic to expect immediate change in campus norms that have evolved over many years. However, understanding the historical development of these norms allows the staff to set in motion activities that, although they may appear to be quite limited at the outset, may be effective over time. Another key to effective change is finding situations when students are in transition, like new student leadership or some other change on campus, and engaging them in a decision that demonstrates the value of their involvement in shaping the campus community. Student energy is captured at an impressionable moment, and a long-term sense that students matter results.

Research and Setting. A meaningful assessment of the campus environment encompasses a comprehensive *resource analysis* including (1) the assessment of the resources available in the institutional environment, (2) the assessment of what resources the intervention will need, (3) an understanding of the resources that need to be generated, and (4) the examination of a process by which the environment can sustain the intervention (Trickett, Kelly, and Vincent, 1985). When the assessment is conducted in such a way, it becomes more than just data collection, it also becomes a viable preventive and developmental intervention.

Turning again to alcohol and drug prevention, one cannot expect a useful assessment of changes in drinking or drug use without understanding the meaning alcohol and other drugs have for the community. To gain such an understanding and achieve research goals, the community's resources must be mobilized. If alcohol or other drug use in the community is researched separately from the meaning such use has for members of the community, the researcher creates an artificial dichotomy between the research and the setting. Furthermore, as the meaning of alcohol and other drug use is exposed, the staff assumes a mediating role between the research and the setting. Thus, in conducting research, the program staff becomes a catalyst for both resource mobilization and change.

Side Effects Research. The ecological paradigm suggests that community research, being itself an intervention, sets in motion other activities that may be as meaningful to the setting as the research findings themselves. For example, there are reports of college administrators who have been reluctant to support alcohol education research for fear that the findings may reflect negatively on the institution (Ingalls, 1982). Campus activities staff can capitalize on such side effects to mobilize campus resources. The possibilities include establishing new forms of communication between previously unconnected resources, developing new policies and procedures for relating to external entities, and improving information management mechanisms. The ability of the researcher to detect and capitalize on the side effects of the research may well determine the extent to which the research achieves its goal of becoming a developmental initiative.

Flexibility in Inquiry. This final principle asserts that ecological inquiry involves a fundamental commitment to flexibility and improvisation. When staff become satisfied with current methods and concepts, opportunities for innovation and improvisation are diminished. Under these circumstances, staff may grow too comfortable with current programmatic approaches. Thus, there is a danger that conservatism and professional orthodoxy may combine to inhibit the process of community development (Trickett, Kelly, and Vincent, 1985). As an ecological consultant on campus, the professional must always be alert to this possibility and seek to keep alive what Trickett and associates have called the "spirit of ecological inquiry."

Conclusion

There is growing consensus that student development efforts must do more than help individual students move from one stage of development to another (Hurst, 1987). Instead, campus activities programs and, especially, involvement initiatives must seek to change the environment so that campus norms and values support student involvement and the sense that students matter. Such social changes are too great a task for any one individual or office acting alone. Individuals responsible for the implementation of student development programs must look beyond the limits of their personal or program resources. They must look at the entire campus as a community rich in resources, which can be mobilized to achieve the goal of change.

The ten principles of community research proposed under the ecological paradigm of Trickett, Kelly, and Vincent (1985) offer a formal set of guidelines that can provide structure to the assessment and implementation of a campus activities program. Under these principles, key activities staff function as ecological consultants on campus. In the ecological paradigm, community assessment and intervention are not seen as separate processes. Instead, they are dynamically and inseparably interactive. While the last three principles specifically address the research relationship, data gathering and community resource mobilization are inherent in the successful application of each principle described. The ecological paradigm has been successfully applied to a variety of social problems, ranging from school reorganization to substance abuse prevention in the community (Kelly and Hess, 1987). It offers a viable model for campus activities staff in their efforts to understand the community and encourage involvement in learning.

References

American Council on Education. *Student Personnel Point of View.* Washington, D.C.: American Council on Education, 1937.

Banning, J. H., and Kaiser, L. "An Ecological Perspective and Model for Campus Design." *Personnel and Guidance Journal,* 1974, *52,* 370-375.

Berkowitz, A. D., and Perkins, H. W. "'Problem Drinking Among College Students: A Review of Recent Research." Paper presented at the annual meeting of the American College Health Association, Washington, D.C., May-June, 1985.

Conyne, R. D., and Clack, R. J. *Environmental Assessment and Design.* New York: Praeger Press, 1981.

Huebner, L. A. "Emerging Issues of Theory and Practice." In L. A. Huebner (ed.), *Redesigning Campus Environments.* New Directions for Student Services, no. 8. San Francisco: Jossey-Bass, 1979.

Hughes, S. D., and Dodder, R. A. "Raising the Minimum Drinking Age: Short-Term Effects with College Student Samples." *Journal of Drug Issues,* 1986, *16,* 609-620.

Hurst, J. C. "Student Development and Campus Ecology: A Rapprochement." *National Association of Student Personnel Administrators Journal,* 1987, *25,* 5-17.

Ingalls, Z. "Higher Education's Drinking Problem." *Chronicle of Higher Education,* July 21, 1982, p. 1.

Kelly, J. G., and Hess, R. E. *The Ecology of Prevention: Illustrating Mental Health Consultation.* New York: Haworth Press, 1987.

Mann, P. A. "Prevention of Child Abuse: Two Contrasting Social Support Services." In J. G. Kelly and R. E. Hess (eds.), *The Ecology of Prevention: Illustrating Mental Health Consultation.* New York: Haworth Press, 1987.

Roberts, D. C. *Student Leadership Programs in Higher Education.* Media Publication. Washington, D.C.: American College Personnel Association, 1980.

Rodgers, R. F. "Theories Underlying Student Development." In D. G. Creamer (ed.), *Student Development in Higher Education: Theories, Practices, and Future Directions.* Media Publication, no. 27. Washington, D.C.: American College Personnel Association, 1980.

Trickett, E. J., Kelly, J. G., and Vincent, T. A. "The Spirit of Ecological Inquiry in Community Research." In E. C. Susskind and D. C. Klein (eds.), *Community Research: Methods, Paradigms, and Applications.* New York: Praeger Press, 1985.

Widick, C., Knefelkamp, L., and Parker, C. "Student Development." In U. Delworth, G. R. Hanson, and Associates (eds.), *Student Services: A Handbook for the Profession.* San Francisco: Jossey-Bass, 1980.

Gerardo M. Gonzalez is associate professor of counselor education at the University of Florida. An authority on alcohol and drug abuse prevention at the college level, he has been nationally involved in program development, research, and policy formulation in these areas.

Student involvement in campus activities needs to be expanded
to include diverse groups of students.

Expanding Participation of Student Subgroups in Campus Activities

Larry J. Ringgenberg

Almost two out of five of today's undergraduates still say
they do not feel a sense of community at their institution.
—Boyer, 1987, p. 191

The student clientele within higher education has been changing during the 1980s. These changes require campus activities staff to deal with the concepts explained in Schlossberg's chapter on mattering. Demographic projections indicate that higher education will serve more minorities, more women, and more older, returning students. Typically, the campus community's response to these groups of students has been either assimilation or separation (Chavez and Carlson, 1986), neither of which contributes to a sense of belonging. All groups of students need to feel that they are important constituencies within the institution and that they matter. This requires that students be empowered to become involved within the campus community.

Empowerment enables students to feel that they are important and that their involvement in campus activities not only benefits the student but contributes to the campus environment. A key factor in empowering

D. C. Roberts (ed.). *Designing Campus Activities to Foster a Sense of Community.*
New Directions for Student Services, no. 48. San Francisco: Jossey-Bass, Winter 1989.

a diverse student population is a warm welcome. Bernard (1981) observed that accepting women to the institution and its programs is not the same as warmly welcoming them.

The call during the 1980s has been for increased pluralism within higher education (Astin, 1983). Pluralism suggests more than merely combining different student subgroups; it also means addressing their special needs and concerns. Further, as these subgroups adapt to the campus community, they should not be forced to give up their history, tradition, and cultural heritage in the interest of creating a student melting pot, which blurs all distinctions among different subgroups. To support the concept of student pluralism is, in effect, to argue that the institution should seek ways to meet the special needs of student subpopulations while fostering a peaceful coexistence among them (Astin, 1983).

A positive climate needs to be developed in which activities that focus on specific groups are considered as important as activities for the traditional population. A climate where differences flourish and are applauded will help eliminate stigmatization. It is unfair to admit minorities—whether of ethnicity, gender, religion, race, or language—only to place them in an environment where they are isolated and left out of the mainstream of social life (Dawson, 1987).

This chapter will review the needs of several types of students, primarily ethnic minority students, whose need for inclusion mirrors the needs of other groups of students.

Student Constituencies

The diversity of students must expand if higher education is to thrive in the coming years. In the near future, minority students will actually outnumber the traditional student population, according to one projection (Carlson and Basler, 1986). This more diverse student population includes ethnic students, women, commuter (part-time) students, older students, and disabled students. Each of these constituencies brings to the campus unique qualities that improve the educational environment. Each faces similar challenges in its attempts to achieve integration into the mainstream of campus life.

Students of color, especially black students, have frequently felt they are not part of the predominantly white campus. Allen (1985) reported that 45 percent of the black undergraduates studied from six predominantly white, state-supported universities felt very little or not at all a part of general campus life. Only 12 percent reported feeling very much a part of social activities on campus.

Campus-life expectations also differ between traditional majority students and black students. White students expect the atmosphere to be conservative regarding social and political issues while liberal regarding personal freedoms. Black students expect just the opposite. This lack of congruence with the predominant campus environment causes immediate discomfort with the campus (Sedlacek, 1987). Hughes (1987) points out that many black students at predominantly white institutions are preoccupied with intellectual survival. They realize that social, personal, emotional, and cultural development will be delayed, not because of an inability to balance academic and social goals but because of the unpreparedness of the institutional environment to plan for and respond to their social and developmental needs.

The importance of involvement has been discussed in the first two chapters. Mallenckrodt and Sedlacek (1985) investigated involvement of minority students at the University of Maryland. They found that the only academic facility related to retention was the library. Use of two nonacademic facilities also predicted retention. These were (1) an outdoor recreation trip sponsored by the union and (2) a campus gymnasium in which students spent two hours per week. Nonacademic variables have been considered prerequisites if black students are to concentrate on academic considerations (Sedlacek and Brooks, 1976; Tracey and Sedlacek, 1984). Critical to becoming involved in the activities of nonacademic facilities is the students' trust level. Participating in activities within nonacademic facilities may demonstrate that students are perceiving themselves as part of the campus community (Mallenckrodt and Sedlacek, 1985).

Minority Participation Committee: An Example of Mattering

The University of Wisconsin system and the University of Wisconsin, La Crosse, have been concerned about minority students and how these students feel about the campus environment. During the spring of 1985, a committee was appointed to assess the accessibility of campus activities to minority students. The committee investigated faculty and staff perceptions of minority student involvement, minority student perceptions of involvement opportunities, and policies and procedures of student organizations that may inhibit involvement of minority students. The minority participation report reviewed the data generated from three instruments (Ringgenberg and Hood, 1988).

Most faculty and staff felt that involvement of minority students was below average compared with traditional students. However, 90 percent of the faculty and staff felt there was open access to campus activities. Some of the faculty qualified their responses by describing "psychological barriers" and the absence of programs to "actively encourage" minority participation. Some of the comments suggested that access was equally available if students only sought involvement. This viewpoint can be perceived as positive; however, it may also typify a majority value structure that says, "Opportunity is all that is required."

Recommendations to increase involvement of minority students asserted the need to do more than encourage students to become involved. Campus activities staff need to court minority students to show them they are needed to make activities meaningful and successful. Minority students should be viewed as a resource through which mainstream groups and students may expand their horizons. Hearty and vigorous recruitment was mentioned often as a method of involving more minority students. Once students are recruited, they need to be welcomed into the organization and provided with meaningful responsibilities, which will make them feel accepted and valuable.

Minority Student Perceptions. The minority student population at La Crosse is composed of students within the following ethnic groups: Native Americans, Asian/Pacific Island Americans (including the Asian refugee populations, such as the Hmong, Cambodian, and Vietnamese), black Americans, and Hispanic Americans. The university has sponsored a variety of services, activities, and organizations to provide support and social experiences for these students. However, it has been noted that many of these students reported a reluctance to seek assistance or to become involved on campus. Involvement was usually limited to their own ethnic organizations.

Among cocurricular programs (dance, intercollegiate athletics, intramurals and recreation, music, sports clubs, and theater), minority student participation in intramurals and recreation was high. In all other areas, however, use and familiarity of the programs was low, and few students said they had been encouraged to become involved. Students would like to have been more involved but were lacking information and encouragement.

The findings in the student governance area (fraternities and sororities, multicultural activities, professional and honorary groups, residence hall government, campus activities programming, and student government itself) were very similar. Familiarity with these groups, except multicultural activities, was very low. Students made it clear that these activities should offer more information and encouragement to minority students.

That less than half of the minority students were familiar with or were participating in organizations and activities is not necessarily a problem in itself. However, combined with the extremely low numbers who have received information or have been encouraged to participate, this fact argues for stronger efforts to reach out to minority students, particularly in student governance, where the numbers are lowest.

Access to Organizations. The third source of information analyzed was the policies and procedures of student organizations, which may inhibit or encourage involvement of minority students. Surveys were sent to all 150 student organizations, including athletic squads; a 42 percent return was received.

Few organizations reported having strategies to encourage participation of minority students. Those organizations that did report such efforts (18 percent) used personal contact with minority students, cosponsorship of programs, and contact with the Minority Affairs Office. In contrast, almost all of the respondents publicized their organization, primarily through word of mouth (91 percent), personal contact (81 percent), and posters (78 percent).

Student organizations have a tendency to become cliquish in that individuals who join them are often friends of current members. Since minority students are not present, a never-ending cycle exists, maintaining the homogeneous membership. The ability to recruit minority students by word of mouth is minimized.

Task Force Recommendations. As a result of reviewing the research just summarized, the Task Force on Minority Involvement concluded with these recommendations:

1. Minority students must be recruited through the use of personal contacts. Only through intensive recruitment, including a position for the recruitment of minority students, can La Crosse increase the pool of these students. The university should initiate and fund a developing leaders program. A number of minority students would get involved in student organizations if their comfort with leadership responsibilities was greater.

2. More information about involvement opportunities should be disseminated to minority students, faculty, and staff. This should include information about grade point average requirements for various organizations.

3. The institution should emphasize the importance of involvement as part of the educational experience at La Crosse.

4. The recruitment of minority students should have high priority.

5. More cooperative programming should occur. This includes cosponsorship of programs with minority student organizations and other departments and organizations.

6. All segments of the institution should assist with programming and advising minority student organizations.

7. Minority student orientation events should stress involvement opportunities and services to students.

8. Faculty and staff should attend programs to heighten their awareness of the issues facing minority students at the university.

9. The financial concerns of minority students should become a concern of the institution. In addition to providing on-campus positions, the institution should work with the La Crosse business community to develop part-time jobs for minority students.

10. Attention should be paid to developing a sense of community for all students at La Crosse. Minority students, in particular, would benefit from closer ties with the institution. Because there is a small minority

population within the city of La Crosse, the institution needs to ensure that minority students can identify with the community.

These recommendations are likely to be similar to those that would emerge at numerous institutions.

A Five-Stage Model

Stewart and Hartt (1987a) have presented a program called OASES, a five-stage model for promoting multiculturalism. The first three stages— Orientation, Affiliation, and Support—systematically attend to adaptation issues. The power gained through adaptive adjustment allows the student to accept the greater challenge of difference provided in the fourth stage—Extension. The last stage, Systemization, has the student interweaving the complexity gained from those challenges into the self.

Stage 1: Orientation. Orientation involves setting norms and providing information and allows for the physical adjustment of new students. Resources should focus on all students, not just resident students. Staff should be wary of potential barriers between different groups of students. In addition, commonalities between groups should be stressed; this will establish a foundation for subsequent exploration of cultural and ethnic differences.

Stage 2: Affiliation. All students have a need to connect with the campus environment through meaningful relationships in organizations and with individuals. Affiliation is an exploratory stage in which students find out about available options and resources. Activities should concentrate on potential common interests students will share despite perceived differences based on race, sex, age, or disability.

Stage 3: Support. Staff members need to support students so they are able to connect with the institution and develop a feeling of fitting into the environment, which in turn will develop into a sense of belonging. Typically, minority students are unable to negotiate through the realm of campus activities, or they are unaware of the resources available in this area. These individuals should know how to access resources and work within the system.

Stage 4: Extension. Individuals want not only to belong but to have pride in their campus affiliations. The extension phase is manifest when student organizations recognize that they are not autonomous entities but parts of a larger community. More cooperative programming occurs at this stage.

Stage 5: Systemization. Individuals begin to examine qualitative variables that encourage integration of persons into the setting. The systemization stage challenges campus organizations and programming committees to establish a sense of community in which events are planned not only for specific groups but with diversity in mind (adapted from Stewart and Hartt, 1987a).

Similarities to Other Constituencies

The common thread that may be used to tie ethnic minority students to women, disabled students, commuter students, and nontraditional-age students is the concept of inclusion. All of these constituencies need to feel that the university or college wants them to be enrolled and that they provide valuable contributions to the learning environment. This is precisely the point made by Schlossberg in identifying the importance of mattering to all students. With students who are perceived to be demographically marginal, mattering becomes even more critical. Each constituency may have special needs, which will serve as focal points or symbols for its inclusion on campus.

Carlson and Basler (1986) point out that women and returning students often have similar needs. This is partially due to the large number of women who make up the returning student population. Linda Reisser (cited in Carlson and Basler, 1986) has identified eight characteristics shared by older students returning to college.

1. They are easily frustrated by the language, procedures, and requirements of higher educational institutions.
2. They are excited about learning and highly motivated, but anxious about their abilities to compete with younger students.
3. They either have very specific career goals or are uncertain about how to relate their abilities and aptitudes to the job market.
4. They are unaware of the variety of nontraditional learning options available, such as independent study, individualized degree programs and credit for experiential learning.
5. They have job and family responsibilities that complicate their academic schedule.
6. They are often at a turning point in their lives, such as a career change, transition from married to single life, or are returning to school after a period of homemaking or part-time work.
7. They are easily alienated by institutional practices that fail to recognize their life experiences, their diverse learning styles and skills, their needs to use time efficiently and to personalize their education, and their special requirements for childcare services, basic learning skills, support groups, and cocurricular activities that complement their interests and needs.
8. They are making significant investments of time and money in order to accomplish educational goals [pp. 53-54].

Returning students and women students need child-care facilities, support groups for themselves and their families, a common gathering ground, and social, recreational, cultural, and educational programs that meet their interests. Some of these programs should focus on family and therefore be appropriate for children. Programming for a family is a great deal different from programming for the traditional-age student.

For example, tastes in music and comedy can be extremely different. However, failure to provide family programming could isolate these students from campus.

Commuter students, as well as the other new constituencies, need someone on campus to be responsible for assisting them. The institution should establish an office at which they can seek help, file complaints, and learn about special programs and services available to them (Boyer, 1987). The National Clearinghouse for Commuter Programs has identified thirty-seven specific activities for commuters, including information centers, off-campus housing referral, car pool assistance, shower facilities, lounges, and special bus service, preferred parking and overnight facilities (Rue and Ludt, 1983).

Disabled students are another population sometimes needing special attention. Typically, institutions have established offices to assist these students, but there is still a danger they will not connect with the rest of the campus. Access to traditional services and programs is crucial for disabled students. Opportunities available to nondisabled students should be accessible to disabled students.

The emphasis with disabled student issues should be on equality. This approach suggests the need to develop educational and awareness programs that address the similarities of all students as well as the unique physical needs of students with disabilities. Students should live together, be served in the same locations, and be able to attend events and activities together. Accessibility removes barriers and draws attention to the similarities rather than the differences among students (Kriegsman and Hershenson, 1987).

Colleges and universities have typically operated from either a monocultural perspective, which expects all students to accept a set of norms based on the institution's traditional value system, or a bicultural approach, which allows the nontraditional student population to exist but in a secondary place with respect to that of the majority culture. The dilemma for campus activities staff is how to create an environment where students share a sense of purpose and unity while still accepting and appreciating individual differences (Stewart and Hartt, 1987b).

Educational Outcomes

Astin's (1984) research on the educational benefits that accrue to students involved in campus activities and campus life has already been mentioned prominently in other chapters. Besides bringing personal benefits, student involvement in the 1990s will positively affect the educational environment. This will especially hold for campus activities, whose informal learning environment, which promotes sharing and interaction over ideas, can utilize the different perspectives brought by different individuals. Campus activities works with academic programs to create a laboratory for experiences, in which students may apply what they learn in the classroom to their duties as student leaders.

This laboratory can embrace a multicultural perspective, which should bring about broadly based educational efforts and policies to increase tolerance and understanding of differences and reduce fear about the "other" (DeCarbo, 1987). Another strength of the institution that values diversity is that exposure to the broadest range of human experience is the only way individuals can be fully educated for the world they inherit. Also, students must confront and be challenged by diverse elements to gain comprehension of others and develop understanding and sensitivity in their relationships. These benefits represent a belief that by favoring and embracing diversity, the institution enriches campus life and makes the experience more wholesome (DeCarbo, 1987).

Empowerment

The concept of empowering students of diverse backgrounds changes the role of the campus activities staff. Empowerment begins the process of re-creating organizations and changing practices so that organizations become more open, reflect many cultures, and embrace students from all backgrounds. Campus activities leaders need to use their power to set standards for inclusion and fairness and for sharing that power (Manning, 1988). Empowerment of student groups requires a proactive approach to involve them in campus activities. This push includes invitations and personal contacts by staff members. It also includes providing these students with evidence that the institution cares about their involvement and their experience. In the process, the college or university demonstrates that students of diverse backgrounds matter. This may include paying attention to their environmental needs, such as lockers for commuter students, office space for nontraditional and ethnic students, escort services for women students, child-care services, and cosponsorship of programs. An environmental concern could even extend to dining options that enable students to eat when they are on campus. The menus would ideally include a variety of foods, reflecting attention to ethnic diversity.

The campus activities staff should meet with the various groups, become available for advising on resources, and assist students in getting involved in mainstream campus activities. Mainstreaming diverse student groups is essential if students are to learn about one another. Mainstreaming works when students have the opportunity and support to learn about one another through shared experiences, to reflect on differences, and to discover common values (Porter, Rosenfield, and Spaull, 1985).

Improving contacts with these groups will only work if continued attention is paid to the traditional student population, with an emphasis on multicultural education. Traditional students must have the opportunity, structure, and reinforcement for replacing stereotypes with personal knowledge, for learning to view differences for their complimentary qualities and their potential to create growth (Porter, Rosenfield, and Spaull, 1985). In short, traditional students should have well-rounded programs that reach out to all student subgroups.

Conclusion

The concept of mattering impacts all students. When students do not believe an institution cares about them, when it does not seem to be listening to their viewpoints or making opportunities available, then student involvement declines and satisfaction with the institution decreases. These qualities of caring and of showing students that they do matter work with traditional students and, perhaps even more effectively, with the subgroups discussed in this chapter.

Boyer (1987) discusses the concept of a community of learners. Higher education needs to develop such a community, in which all members feel valuable and in which administration, faculty, and staff are not only concerned with students but with each other. This is especially important since modeling behavior is an important process of education. "At a time when social bonds are tenuous, students during their collegiate years should discover the reality of their dependency on each other. They must understand what it means to share and sustain traditions. Community must be built" (p. 195).

Diversity has become the rallying cry for the late 1980s. Attempts are being made to bring more minority students, disabled students, commuter students, and other nontraditional groups into the campus environment. This cry for diversity will not be met by merely bringing these groups to campus. They need to be included in the mainstream of the campus environment. In turn this inclusion will result in a cultural broadening of all students.

References

Allen, W. R. "Black Student, White Campus: Structural, Interpersonal, and Psychological Correlates of Success." *Journal of Negro Education*, 1985, *54*, 134-137.
Astin, A. W. "A Look at Pluralism in the Contemporary Student Population." Address given to the Iowa State University Student Affairs Summer Institute, Ames, Iowa, July 1983.
Astin, A. W. "Student Involvement: A Developmental Theory for Higher Education." *Journal of College Student Personnel*, 1984, *24*, 297-308.
Astin, A. W. *Achieving Educational Excellence: A Critical Assessment of Priorities and Practices in Higher Education.* San Francisco: Jossey-Bass, 1985.

Bernard, J. "Women's Educational Needs." In A. W. Chickering (ed.), *The Modern American College: Responding to the New Realities of Diverse Students and a Changing Society*. San Francisco: Jossey-Bass, 1981.

Boyer, E. L. *College: The Undergraduate Experience in America*. New York: Harper & Row, 1987.

Carlson, J. M., and Basler, M. "The Quiet Revolution: Student Activities and the Nontraditional Student." *Campus Activities Programming*, 1986, *19* (6), 52-56.

Chavez, E., and Carlson, J. "Building a Multicultural Environment." *Bulletin of the Association of College Unions-International*, 1986, *53* (5), 4-6.

Dawson, M. E. "The Mandate for Multiculturalism." In *Boston 1987: Our Town Meeting*. Bloomington, Ind.: Association of College Unions–International, 1987.

DeCarbo, E. "Diversity and the International Community: Mobilizing the Resource." *Campus Activities Programming*, 1987, *19* (9), 51-55.

Hughes, M. S. "Black Students' Participation in Higher Education." *Journal of College Student Personnel*, 1987, *26* (6), 523-545.

Kriegsman, K. H., and Hershenson, D. B. "A Comparison of Ablebodied and Disabled College Students on Erickson's Ego Stages and Maslow's Need Levels." *Journal of College Student Personnel*, 1987, *28* (1), 48-53.

Mallenckrodt, B., and Sedlacek, W. *Student Retention and Use of Campus Facilities*. Research Report, no. 8. College Park: University of Maryland, 1985.

Manning, K. "The Multi-Cultural Challenge of the 1990s." *Campus Activities Programming*, 1988, *21* (3), 52-57.

Porter J., Rosenfield, E., and Spaull, E. "Tapping Diversity Within Higher Education: Some Lessons Learned." *Association on Handicapped Student Service Programs in Post-Secondary Education Bulletin*, 1985, *3*, 70-86.

Ringgenberg, L., and Hood, T. *Report on Minority Student Participation at the University of Wisconsin–La Crosse*. La Crosse: University of Wisconsin, 1988.

Rue, P., and Ludt, J. "Organizing for Commuter Student Services." In S. S. Stewart (ed.), *Commuter Students: Enhancing Their Educational Experiences*. New Directions for Student Services, no. 27. San Francisco: Jossey-Bass, 1983.

Sedlacek, W. E. "Black Students on White Campuses: Twenty Years of Research." *Journal of College Student Personnel*, 1987, *28* (6), 484-495.

Sedlacek, W. E., and Brooks, G. C., Jr. *Racism in American Education: A Model for Change*. Chicago: Nelson-Hall, 1976.

Stewart, G. M., and Hartt, J. A. "Promoting a Multicultural Environment Through College Activities, Services, and Programs." In *Boston 1987: Our Town Meeting*. Bloomington, Ind.: Association of College Unions–International, 1987a.

Stewart, G. M., and Hartt, J. A. "Multiculturalism: A Community Among Differences." *Bulletin of the Association of College Unions–International*, 1987b, *55*, 4-8.

Tracey, T. J., and Sedlacek, W. E. "Noncognitive Variables in Predicting Academic Success by Race." *Measurement and Evaluation in Guidance*, 1984, *16*, 171-178.

Larry J. Ringgenberg is associate director of student activities and centers at the University of Wisconsin, La Crosse, and is on the teaching faculty in the College Student Personnel program. He has served for three years on the task force on minority student participation.

A cooperative, integrative approach to campus activities
provides significant opportunities for student growth and
community building.

Campus Activities
Coordination

Donald B. Mills

The college campus is a thriving, bustling place. An independent observer would notice many student activities. But the same person might also comment that these activities seem independent of each other. Such observations are frequently on target. The campus is teeming with activities—classes, meetings, programs, and events. But are they related and should they be?

This chapter will discuss campus activities, the relationships between activities, and one concept for connecting disparate activities. College students could acquire a common body of skills and knowledge from campus activities as easily as they do from shared academic majors. Furthermore, the integration of activities creates an environment where students are shown they matter. Campus activities coordination becomes central to preparing students for citizenship.

The literature does not provide a clear definition of student activities; rather, it suggests objectives. Mueller (1961) believed that a student's development is enhanced by activities that are successful in "complementing classroom instruction or enhancing academic learning; developing social-interaction; providing for a profitable use of leisure time; and encouraging better values and higher standards" (p. 275). Shaffer and Martinson (1966) suggested a fifth category for activities that lead to a student's

D. C. Roberts (ed.). *Designing Campus Activities to Foster a Sense of Community.*
New Directions for Student Services, no. 48. San Francisco: Jossey-Bass, Winter 1989.

participation as a responsible citizen. More recently McKaig and Policello (1979) have indicated: "The organization of student activities on college and university campuses has taken many administrative forms. As a consequence, a consensually validated description of a student activities unit does not exist" (p. 95). Lee Upcraft (1985) has indicated that a broad-based, vigorous campus activities program enhances retention and student satisfaction.

Traditional campus activities are no longer the high-demand activities they once were. While recent information indicates renewed student interest in community service activities (Theus, 1988), student interest in personal activities, career, and interest groups is growing. In addition, many activities aim at the traditional college student, who represents a decreasing percentage of students attending colleges and universities (Garland, 1985).

The traditional campus offers a variety of activities and formats supervised from different offices. Lectures, films, social events, student organizations, student government, career fairs, health-promotion events, and concerts are a few examples of the programs offered in the hope that students will find activities to match their needs. This is reminiscent of a smorgasbord: lots of choices with no assurance for balanced nutrition.

Another approach is to coordinate activities and have a sense of desired outcomes. While administrators know that activities will occur on campus, they are frequently silent on the mission of the overall program or the benefits that will accrue to participating students. Garland (1985) indicates that student affairs professionals have a unique opportunity to become "integrators" of the perspectives and subsystems at work on the college campus.

By coordinating activities across departmental lines, staff can meet students' needs. Rather than leaving students on their own to select helpful activities, the coordinative approach designs activities to meet students' overall educational goals while assisting in the achievement of institutional objectives.

The coordination of activities allows students to engage the environment in meaningful ways. By using a coordinative approach, students recognize the legitimacy of their needs. This recognition of an environment designed to focus on needs leads students to a sense of significance and a feeling of mattering.

Administration of Campus Activities

Higher education institutions are organized along functional lines not dissimilar to those of business. The obvious advantage to a functional organization is its convenience for administrators. The focus on function allows an institution to specialize within units. The creation of specialties enables practitioners to build a separate language and goal structure within the larger institutional structure. However, while specialties enable practitioners to focus on function, they do not emphasize the quality of the outcome.

Having a clear understanding of special functions provides fertile ground for justifying training programs for new professionals. The circle then becomes complete, specialties become more arcane, and functions are redefined. The training of specialists assures departmental autonomy. It also guarantees an approach based on the presentation of campus activities rather than their effects. University administrators appreciate a functional approach since it simplifies methods of program definition and evaluation. Funding issues are more easily solved and assignments of responsibility more easily made when function is the central criterion for evaluation.

In business organizations, focusing on the product has clear advantages. However, in student affairs it may be a disadvantage to remove the focus from the student. In the student view the university is designed to help attain goals. Students do not attend college for a housing experience or a student government experience. The expectation is for a total institutional experience.

The college student seeking involvement on a campus searches for activities that assist in meeting educational goals. The involvement is with the institution; the student uses departments or units as tools, which play no functional role from the student's perspective except to be supportive. Therefore, an activity administration working to build community must recognize that students view activities as a unified whole. And since they do not view themselves as a series of separate entities, activities must mirror that perception.

Thematic Rationale for Activities Coordination

Appropriate coordination of activities depends primarily on a philosophical integration of student affairs units. This requires an understanding of desired outcomes from campus activities as they relate to meeting student needs and goals. Consistency among units that offer activity programs assures that desired outcomes will occur regardless of which activities are chosen or which unit may sponsor them. Peters and Austin (1985) indicate, "As the best companies are imbued with philosophies, so apparently are the best schools" (p. 397). The philosophy of one school states: "Education presumes a climate of care. [The school] must be a kind of home which offers its inhabitants a sense of belonging, of individuality strengthened by expectation, of security born of respect" (p. 395).

The integrated, cooperative effort has an effect beyond the assurance of consistency. Moving beyond specialization benefits activity administrators as well. It is likely to enhance support between units, develop morale within units and student affairs divisions, and build creativity. The sense of mattering in staff is improved as well as the delivery of programming to students.

The selection of a philosophical basis for activities coordination is a serious process. To properly make the selection, staff must be cognizant of institutional, divisional, and unit goals; they must understand the student body and the subgroups within it. This assumes that there are methods in place to adequately evaluate student needs and to assess both staff and financial resources. It further requires a staff committed to the growth and development of students within a changing environment. Jacobi, Astin, and Ayala (1987) indicate: "A principal concept in [student development] theory is that of student involvement, the time and the physical and psychological energy that the student invests in the academic experience. The more students are involved in the academic experience, the greater their learning and growth and the more fully their talents are likely to develop. The less they are involved, the less they learn and the greater the chances they will become dissatisfied and drop out" (pp. 17–18).

The challenge is clear. Student involvement must precede desired outcomes, and the burden falls squarely on units sponsoring activities to attract students to these activities and see that outcomes are related to both institutional and student goals. Clearly staffs must work together and be mutually supportive to be successful in meeting the challenge.

Several philosophical bases of program coordination are easily determined. It should be remembered that philosophical foundations should not be designed to define particular activity programs. Rather, they should define the thematic rationale of activities. Within that rationale specific activities are offered to meet goals appropriate to the participating population. One thematic basis for coordination is multicultural education. Here the opportunities for student involvement are numerous. A common theme can be threaded through several traditional student affairs units, including international student affairs, student activities, intercultural development, residential living, career planning, and Greek affairs. The theme can be exploited while engaging in traditional activities. Students begin to appreciate the transferability of skills and knowledge between settings and progress toward the accomplishment of their developmental goals.

Wellness provides another thematic approach to integrating activities of different units. By using an integrated approach to wellness education and activities, the holistic approach to life-style education transcends individual unit lines. In the wellness example it is possible to join academic and student affairs units in partnership. In addition, the wellness approach to healthy life-styles in all dimensions of a person's life enables students to engage the concept in multiple settings and at multiple levels of complexity.

On many campuses leadership programs and the development of leadership skills are being used as philosophical bases for cooperative programming. Again, students can frequently practice these skills while engaged in traditional activities. As they progress through an institution, their involvement in leadership programs becomes more significant and has a greater impact on the institution itself, whether through organizational leadership or, perhaps, the acceptance of paraprofessional employment opportunities. In any case the development of leaders provides students with skills that are useful not only beyond the immediate environment but to the present community as well.

The examples just listed are not exhaustive, but they do illustrate that an institution can provide consistent philosophical approaches to the campus environment and meet developmental needs of students. Student affairs also benefits. One of the stereotypes used to define campus activities is that it is the "fun and games" department. Significant educational enterprises occur in academic areas whereas campus activities are designed to entertain and occupy. The concentration on desirable outcomes based on a philosophical integration of institutional units mandates a new look at campus activities as serious tools in education.

Design of Activities Coordination

Typically, activity programs are planned and implemented by institutional units to further their goals. Student involvement occurs when students associate with a unit and choose to participate. While this approach benefits program planning and participation, it may only tangentially include those who would ultimately wish to participate.

In a cooperative, integrated program, relationships are created between existing student affairs units, between student affairs units and academic departments, and between student affairs units and organized student groups. Program success requires using *student-determined groups* as a basis for planning and implementation. Susan Batchelor, director of student activities at Texas Christian University, assisted in the conceptualization of this approach. We maintain that while the institution is organized for its convenience, students will select activities based on their interest in certain student groups. Marketing to an entire institutional population is frequently an inefficient and even ineffective method of providing services and programs across the entire range of student needs and goals. However, basing implementation on student-determined groups allows considerably more specificity in marketing programs and services. Clearly opportunity to focus on the developmental characteristics of students is greater when a common basis for participation exists.

Several types of student-determined groups come easily to mind. Residence-based student groups offer an entrée to a wide range of students. Residents may be grouped by classification, special interests, major, or random assignment. They may be campus residents or commuters. But the key is to involve an already established base, where students are comfortable and have some control over the environment.

Student governance groups offer extensive opportunities for theme-based, cooperative activities. No single student organization encompasses the breadth of the student body as completely as governance organizations. Not only do these groups engage in legislative functions but their membership has access to the entire student population. Many opportunities exist to identify student interests as well as existing vehicles to meet those interests.

Other examples of existing student-determined groups include Greek organizations, religious organizations, honor societies, academically based interest groups, and subpopulations of the student body, such as commuters, graduate students, international students, and married students. The common feature of all these organizations is membership based on common interest. In summary, a theme base for programming can philosophically and practically be focused on the specific needs of students in their environment.

Opportunities for Student Involvement

Obviously not all programs are suitable to the model being suggested here. Certain activities and programs are unique to specific departments and do not lend themselves to integration with other departments or have the need for consistency among departments. Those which come to mind include certain campus rituals or traditional events, activities that have a specific and linear function (for example, job placement interviews), and student-initiated functions such as social events. But several types of programs do lend themselves to coordination among units. For example, leadership programs can be coordinated with residence hall groups, Greek organizations, or other student activity groups. Persons who have developed leadership skills could become part of a pool of students available for leadership positions. Leadership skills could be reported assets for students taking part in placement activities. In short, leadership programming provides skills that can be transferred to a variety of environments.

As a thematic approach, leadership can be emphasized in speaker programs, retreats and seminars, academic offerings, and recruitment. The thematic program emphasizes not only the desired developmental goal but the functional utility of an activity. Thus, although leadership may be a theme, it is not necessarily the focus of an activity. This further underscores the need to use student-determined groups as a basis for participation whenever possible.

The criteria for selection of a theme such as leadership is its relationship to developmental opportunities for students. Chickering's (1969) vectors of change among college students are well known. He states: "Colleges and universities will dominate [students'] waking hours and determine the behaviors they pursue, the thoughts they consider, the attitudes they question or accept, the future directions they take, the lifestyles they develop. There is no question about this. The only question is whether rational response will be made to enable more effective development along all seven vectors of change, or whether these vectors will continue largely ignored, incidentally fostered or hampered as by-products of other decisions" (p. 289). The intentional focus on development and the rational understanding of present developmental status among students guide program selection.

Astin (1977) indicates that students' achievements are affected by a variety of environmental experiences. The role of the activity programmer is to assure that students interact with their environments. He presents further recommendations, as noted earlier by Schlossberg, which suggest that involvement will not only encourage student persistence, it will intensify the undergraduate experience. The conscious effort to increase student involvement also enhances the establishment of community. However, a true sense of community is only possible with effective coordination. The sense of community flourishes among program planners and is further translated to students, who develop a sense of continuity in the institution, of belonging to an important enterprise, and of being at the center of the institution in both structured academic and activity programs. Additionally, the relationship between academic and activity programs is enhanced.

Activities Center

The intentional, cooperative effort to maintain a unified thematic program does require some organizational considerations. One method of organizing that offers several benefits emerges from the concept of an *activities center*. The activities center may be a physical location although it is more a philosophical concept than a place. Nevertheless, a physical location provides the institutional community—both students and staff— with a locus of activities. Cooperation depends on a coherent centralization of information and a means to focus on activities and their outcomes. Ideally, the activities center should be a reporting unit to the dean or vice president so that its role as a coordinating office may be enhanced.

In addition, the center assumes the calendaring function of the cooperative efforts. Calendaring becomes important not only to avoid conflicting dates and to provide scheduling but to prevent duplication of efforts, to assure a rational order of presentation of programs based on student development theory, and to assure breadth of services to the entire student body. This last function maintains the sense of a broad-based community and the participation of a breadth of student-determined groups.

In a philosophical sense the center adopts a role similar to that of a project manager in a business enterprise. While specialists plan and execute activities, the staff of the center oversee and evaluate. While deciding which theme-based programs will be the focus of cooperative, integrative efforts is a concern of all student affairs staffs, the responsibility for program assurance falls to the activities center staff.

The staff, therefore, of the activities center have some unique responsibilities. While the staffs of all units in the integrative effort must take a broad view of the educational goals of activities, the abilities of specialists are still required. However, the staff of the activities center must understand not only the presentation of various activities but the expected outcomes of all activities, their contributions to student development, and the methods of evaluation. The orientation and training of staff should stress these areas.

Staff should include not only professionals but student paraprofessionals, clericals, and volunteers. All staff must demonstrate creativity, flexibility, and a genuine interest in student growth. The activities center becomes a focal point for student referral to specific organizations and programs. It will have knowledge of related academic offerings and will generate information regarding program success. The staff then will have much student contact and must be knowledgeable and helpful. Variety in staff backgrounds will assure the comfort of all students entering the activities center environment.

Even if a physical location is not available for the activities center, the concept provides a centrality for student opportunities. Opportunities for leadership—whether in student groups, campus committees, or even off campus—will be known to students through the center. Work opportunities may also be coordinated through the center, particularly paraprofessional staff opportunities. Students can receive common training and then be referred to units that need professional-level skills. Individual units can then train students in specialized skills.

In short, the organization of an activities center involves students in the campus and in their own education. It has the potential to increase retention, which in turn enhances community development. In addition, it recognizes the important role of students in maintaining campus activities. Since the cooperative effort to integrate campus activities is based on student-determined groups, activity center staff must have a close relationship to student governance and to student organizations. To do otherwise would limit the effectiveness of the activities center and erect communication barriers with students. Effective marketing of integrative programs demands effective communication, as does the creation of community.

Summary

The creation and maintenance of a campus community requires that students be meaningfully involved in the campus environment. This involvement should be structured to foster student development and to meet educational goals, which can be accomplished through the integration of thematic programming throughout student affairs units.

While traditional campus activities tend to be organized by function, this chapter has suggested that organization be geared to the achievement of student development goals and competencies. Students should understand their involvement in activities as part of their preparation for life beyond college. By providing an appropriate philosophical basis for activities, the institution's resources are used to their fullest extent to meet student needs and goals. The use of student-determined groups enhances the ability to create community within the student population. In addition, a cooperative effort among units offering activities creates a sense of community and significance among the participating staffs.

The activities center concept maintains a unified, cooperative effort. By centralizing activities, the concept allows students to see the institution as a whole. Furthermore, activities can be evaluated by outcome. This concept enables students to more easily interact and to take an active part in their learning.

References

Astin, A. W. *Four Critical Years: Effects of College on Beliefs, Attitudes, and Knowledge.* San Francisco: Jossey-Bass, 1977.
Chickering, A. W. *Education and Identity.* San Francisco: Jossey-Bass, 1969.
Garland, P. H. *Serving More Than Students: A Critical Need for College Student Personnel Services.* ASHE-ERIC Higher Education Report, no. 7. Washington, D.C.: Association of the Study of Higher Education, 1985.
Jacobi, M., Astin, A., and Ayala, F. *College Student Outcomes Assessment: A Talent Development Perspective.* ASHE-ERIC Higher Education Report, no. 7. Washington, D.C.: Association for the Study of Higher Education, 1987.
McKaig, R. N., and Policello, S. M. "Student Activities." In G. Kuh (ed.), *Evaluation in Higher Education.* Washington, D.C.: American College Personnel Association, 1979.
Mueller, K. H. *Student Personnel Work in Higher Education.* Boston: Houghton Mifflin, 1961.
Peters, T., and Austin, N. *A Passion for Excellence.* New York: Random House, 1985.
Shaffer, R. H., and Martinson, W. D. *Student Personnel Services in Higher Education.* New York: Center for Applied Research in Education, 1966.

48

Theus, K. T. "Campus-Based Community Service." *Change,* 1988, *20* (5), 27–38.

Upcraft, L. "Residence Halls and Student Activities." In L. Noel, R. Levitz, D. Saluri, and Associates (eds.), *Increasing Student Retention: Effective Programs and Practices for Reducing the Dropout Rate.* San Francisco: Jossey-Bass, 1985.

Donald B. Mills is assistant vice-chancellor for student affairs at Texas Christian University in Fort Worth, Texas.

Building community through the development of partnerships between student affairs and academic affairs will assist campuses in creating a sense of mattering among students, faculty, and student affairs professionals.

Creating Educational Partnerships Between Academic and Student Affairs

William Zeller, John Hinni, James Eison

Exciting developments now occurring in higher education will have significant implications for student personnel throughout the 1990s. Many of these changes focus on building a stronger sense of community on college and university campuses. Developing links between academic and student affairs is one means of strengthening this sense of community. By developing community both inside and outside the classroom, an institution fosters a stronger sense of mattering among students, faculty, and student personnel.

Many leaders in higher education (for example, Astin, 1985; Boyer, 1986; Kuh, Shedd, and Whitt, 1987; Smith, 1982) advocate the creation of stronger communities through the development of common curricular and cocurricular objectives for student life. In *College: The Undergraduate Experience in America,* Boyer (1986) and his study group found "a great separation—sometimes to the point of isolation—between academic and social life on campus" (p. 5). The group concluded that "the college of quality remains a place where the curricular and cocurricular are viewed as having a relationship to each other" (p. 195).

This chapter will outline these trends, discuss barriers that inhibit

D. C. Roberts (ed.). *Designing Campus Activities to Foster a Sense of Community.*
New Directions for Student Services, no. 48. San Francisco: Jossey-Bass, Winter 1989.

the development of curricular-cocurricular links, and describe strategies that Southeast Missouri State University is taking to create partnerships between academic and student affairs.

Trends Supporting Educational Partnerships

Building educational partnerships between academic and student affairs has been an often-stated aspiration of student affairs professionals (American Council on Education, 1937; Bowen, 1977; Miller and Prince, 1977). These aspirations, however, have not been shared by most faculty colleagues. Despite this reality, based on the findings and recommendations of several recent reports in higher education (for example, Boyer, 1986; Study Group on the Conditions of Excellence in American Higher Education, 1984), there now appears to be heightened interest in creating links between the two areas.

Further support for the belief that establishing interdivisional linkages will lead to an enhanced sense of community can be found in the following four educational trends, which are discussed below:

- Renewed interest in promoting educational goals outside the classroom
- Renewed interest in enhancing teaching and learning inside the classroom
- Renewed interest in restoring the role of general and liberal education in the curriculum
- Increased emphasis on active involvement throughout undergraduate education.

Promoting Educational Goals Outside the Classroom. A college or university education should encompass more than the formal academic curriculum. An ever-increasing emphasis is being placed upon the educational value of campus activities and services outside the classroom. As Boyer (1986) stated: "Colleges like to speak of the campus as community, and yet what is being learned in most residence halls today has little connection to the classrooms, indeed, it may undermine the educational purposes of the college. . . . A question that must be asked is, 'How can life outside the classroom support the educational mission of the college?' " (p. 5).

Enhancing Teaching and Learning Inside the Classroom. Recent national reports (Association of American Colleges, 1985; Chickering and Gamson, 1987) emphasize effective teaching strategies as indicators of educational quality. Astin (1985) has questioned the appropriateness of traditional criteria, such as securing resources and research awards, as measures of institutional quality. He has argued that traditional assumptions about excellence often work against real educational values and priorities. Alternatively, he advocates a view of excellence that stresses the intellectual and personal development of students. Effective teaching strategies and the quality of learning and personal development that occur in the classroom should be given high priority when judging institutional excellence.

Restoring General and Liberal Education. The last decade has seen a resurgent interest in general and liberal education. On many campuses this interest has focused on developing students' abilities to integrate and synthesize knowledge to adapt to a changing society. Recently it has been estimated that 80 percent of colleges and universities have revised or are currently revising the general education component of their curricula (Chandler, 1987).

In *Increasing Student Competence and Persistence,* Forrest (1982) recommended that "institutions view general education as being composed of more than just curriculum. . . . How courses are taught, the kind of advice students receive about courses, and what happens to students outside the classroom are important factors in assisting or inhibiting student achievement of the intended outcomes of general education" (p. 3).

Kuh, Shedd, and Whitt (1987) have argued convincingly that liberal education and student affairs programs share a common purpose. They state that "proponents of higher education and champions of student affairs work seem to agree that higher education should address the development of students' personal identity, interpersonal skills and aesthetic sensibilities in addition to intellectual and academic skills" (p. 255).

These thoughts echo those of Berg (1983), who stated: "To educate liberally, learning experiences must be offered which facilitate the maturity of the whole person and enhance development of intellectual maturity. These are goals of student development and clearly they are consistent with the mission and goals of liberal education" (p. 12).

Active Involvement Throughout Undergraduate Education. Many of today's leaders in higher education (for example, Chickering and Gamson, 1987; Cross, 1987) have been outspoken advocates of active learning and involvement opportunities for undergraduates. The Task Group on General Education of the Association of American Colleges (1988) states, "The sort of teaching we propose requires that we encourage active learning and that we become knowledgeable about the ways in which our students hear, understand, interpret and integrate ideas" (p. 28).

The National Institute of Education's report *Involvement in Learning* (Study Group . . . , 1984) states, "The more time and effort students invest in the learning process and the more intensely they engage in their own education, the greater will be their educational experience, and their persistence in college, and the more likely they are to continue their learning" (p. 17). Astin (1985) has made similar claims. For these reasons institutions should provide opportunities for students to be actively involved in their education both inside and outside the classroom.

These four trends will have significant implications for student affairs programs in the future. Furthermore, the justification for creating campus-wide curricular-cocurricular partnerships is compelling. Why then are links between academic divisions and student affairs divisions so difficult to establish? We believe that on most college campuses the creation of links and the development of community is inhibited by a series of barriers. To create successful partnerships, campus personnel must identify these obstacles and design strategies to overcome them.

Identifying Institutional Barriers

Faculty Barriers. Faculty perceptions all too often create interdivisional barriers. Most faculty view their primary function as transmitting knowledge about their discipline. Among faculty on campuses with a research emphasis is the equally powerful belief that a faculty member's primary role is to "create" knowledge. As a result, for most faculty other educational goals of the institution are of secondary importance.

Many faculty identify strongly with their academic departments while they do not with the larger campus community. This may inhibit a strong sense of mattering within the context of the larger community and may in fact create feelings of marginality. A common and related faculty viewpoint is that the only learning of "real significance" occurs in the classroom. Other campus activities that divert students' time, energy, or attention away from their classwork are consequently viewed with suspicion.

A second barrier to the creation of partnerships arises from the many demands made on the faculty's time. Faculty often judge the value of an activity by the degree to which their participation will be favorably regarded by colleagues and administrators in terms of tenure, promotion, and the enhancement of professional reputation. When faculty perform this type of reward-cost analysis, participation in collaborative activities with student affairs staff is typically seen as having little potential for reward, while the possible cost is often viewed as being quite high.

A third barrier is that many faculty do not know or adequately understand the goals of their campus' student affairs division. Most realize, however, that their department competes with "these people" for its share of the institution's financial resources. A fourth barrier is that faculty are generally unaware how cocurricular experiences can improve academic outcomes. Finally, as with other campus constituencies, faculty fear and resist many departures from the traditional. Innovation to create community involves uncertainty and risk.

Student Affairs Barriers. Perceptions commonly held by student affairs staff may also create barriers to curricular-cocurricular partnerships. The view that fostering students' personal development is as important a university function as promoting intellectual growth may create barriers with faculty, who have a different orientation.

A second barrier is that many student affairs staff have neither doctorates nor significant teaching experience. A perceived status differential may lead these staff to view themselves as unequal or as junior partners on campus. This perception is often reinforced, either implicitly or explicitly, by the actions of faculty members.

A third significant barrier is created when faculty efforts to redesign academic programs take place without discussing the impact on the student affairs division. Along similar lines, Creeden (1988) offers insights into eight additional barriers (for example, the attitude that "the only people around here who care about students are student personnel staff" and that "faculty do not work as hard as we do. They are never in their offices").

Successfully Overcoming Barriers

Once barriers have been identified, strategies to overcome them should be developed. We recommend consideration of the following eight strategies:

Recognize Faculty Values. Student affairs programs designed to form links to the academic division will produce less faculty resistance when they are consistent with the faculty-held values of intellectual growth and personal discipline. Faculty will better receive collaborative activities designed to enhance student learning than programs to make college more enjoyable.

Seek Ways to Improve Communication. Many faculty impressions about student affairs professionals were formed during their undergraduate experiences. Similarly the impressions many student affairs professionals hold about faculty were molded by their undergraduate classroom experiences. In both instances negative impressions and prejudices can interfere with communication between these two groups. For these reasons careful attention must be paid to the communication process and strategies must be developed to facilitate each group's talking and working with the other. Faculty do not often create these opportunities; therefore, student affairs staff must usually take the initiative.

Use Time Wisely. When faculty and student affairs professionals attempt to work together, they must remember that time wasted in poorly run meetings can produce ill feelings. Meetings must be clearly planned; they should yield active plans and expected outcomes. It is especially important that participants experience the positive feelings associated with productive activity early in the process.

Use Academic Programs as a Springboard for Creating Partnerships. Faculty resistance to change or innovation will be minimized when academic programs provide the foundation for new student affairs programs. Later, we will describe how this recommendation has successfully guided our actions at Southeast Missouri State University.

Create Positive Visibility on Campus. The more familiar the campus community becomes with an idea, the less resistance it offers. It is risky, however, to publicize plans for new and innovative programs before a proposal has been approved through the usual chain of command. Once approved, however, new programs should receive campus-wide publicity.

Sponsor Periodic Professional Development Programs. Seminars and workshops can raise consciousness and build skills. Such programs should include both faculty and student affairs professionals and provide participants frequent opportunities for collaboration.

Encourage Qualified Student Affairs Staff to Seek Adjunct Faculty Appointments. When student affairs professionals provide qualified classroom instruction and interact with faculty in professional activities, their credibility is enhanced. Selection procedures must of course meet institutional criteria for faculty appointment.

Find Ways to Reward Faculty Involvement in Cocurricular Activities. All too often institutions do not adequately reward teaching excellence; thus, it is not surprising that faculty involvement in educational activities outside the classroom typically receives insignificant attention. Though difficult to address, these activities should be given prominence in faculty reward systems.

Liberal Education at Southeast Missouri State University

Southeast Missouri State University has recently begun implementing a liberal education program entitled University Studies. This forty-eight–semester-hour program, developed over a ten-year period, consists of over seventy new courses. The unifying theme of the new program is "Enhancing the Humanity of the Student."

Program Highlights. The following nine objectives provide the central focus for instruction within each new course. Students will demonstrate

- The ability to locate and gather information
- Capabilities for critical thinking, reasoning, and analyzing
- Effective communication skills
- An understanding of human experiences and the ability to relate them to the present
- An understanding of various cultures and their interrelationships
- The ability to integrate the breadth and diversity of knowledge and experience
- The ability to make informed, intelligent value decisions
- The ability to make informed, sensitive esthetic responses

- The ability to function responsibly in one's natural, social, and political environment.

One requirement of the University Studies program is an introductory course for freshmen. While many institutions have freshman experience courses similar to the one pioneered by John Gardner at the University of South Carolina, Columbia, few institutions require participation by all beginning students. The syllabus for the introductory course was formally approved by all five colleges in the university and has been refined through two semesters of pilot testing. This course is discussion- and writing-intensive and employs active learning strategies to introduce students to the university experience (both curricular and cocurricular) in general and the University Studies program in particular.

Another feature of the program is a group of three upper-level interdisciplinary courses. One of these courses will be taught as a senior seminar and will require a written and oral report based upon research using the methods of more than one discipline. Although significant barriers to the development of community still exist on our campus, specific initiatives have been taken to link the learning objectives of student affairs with those of the new University Studies program.

Creating Educational Partnerships. The new University Studies program at Southeast Missouri State generated considerable interest within the Division of Student Services. It was apparent that the program's nine general education objectives could provide a foundation not only for curricular programs but for complementary cocurricular learning opportunities. A task force was created to develop comprehensive cocurricular program initiatives that were linked to curricular programs. The ultimate objective was to create a "community of learning" on campus in which life outside the classroom would complement what was happening in the classroom. Over a two-year period, the task force developed a number of new program offerings within the division; nine of these are highlighted below.

University Studies Resource Manual. The Student Services University Studies Resource Manual was created through the combined effort of the individual departments within the division. This manual contains (1) a divisional mission statement, which incorporates the educational concepts of the University Studies program, (2) mission statements for each department in student services, (3) a comprehensive listing of over 127 student affairs programs, and (4) a description of the educational skills and learning opportunities addressed in each program. This manual has been distributed to each of the departments in student services, the University Studies office, the provost, and the academic deans. The manual will be revised and updated annually.

Cocurricular Bulletin. Following the assessment of current offerings, the task force planned initiatives to further enhance the cocurricular activities sponsored by the division. The task force concluded that the division lacked an effective means to communicate the activities, programs, and services that are offered to students. A cocurricular bulletin was developed to provide concise information about activities, organizations, clubs, leadership positions, and so on. The bulletin enables students to develop a plan of involvement throughout their undergraduate years. In addition, a record of involvement was developed to formally record a student's activities on campus. This record can be placed in the student's career placement credentials file during the senior year.

Student Activities Calendar. The division also lacked a method for compiling and communicating upcoming events and programs on campus. Many introductory course faculty hope to encourage increased student attendance at selected cocurricular activities. A mainframe computer program has been developed to create a program calendar. This calendar will be distributed weekly to faculty and staff.

Independent Study and Practicum Opportunities. The task force determined that meaningful educational partnerships could be developed between academic and student affairs by providing opportunities for juniors and seniors to participate in practicums or independent studies within selected student affairs departments. Interested students would be responsible for designing and proposing their projects. Independent studies have already been developed in the Departments of Mass Communications, Teacher Education, Management, Interior Design, and Political Science. A brochure and guidelines have been written to publicize these opportunities to students and faculty. One benefit of this program that has already been observed has been the increased communication between student affairs and academic affairs. In addition, it is hoped that students will develop stronger identification with various campus offices, thus enhancing their sense of mattering.

Paraprofessional/Peer Adviser Program. One of the most intensive opportunities for cocurricular skill development for students on our campus is the paraprofessional position. Resident adviser, peer adviser, career planning adviser, orientation co-leader, and academic tutor are positions that have been offered to upper-level students. The comprehensive training that students receive and the responsibilities associated with these positions help students to develop and practice skills in communications, cross-cultural awareness, decision making, problem solving, and leadership. A new comprehensive training model has been developed for the resident adviser position. The model uses the University Studies objectives as a foundation for training. A credit-bearing class for first-year resident advisers has been offered. A workbook is now being developed for this class; each of its nine chapters will concentrate on one of the University Studies objectives.

Assessment and Outcome Measures. Assessing the learning and skill development that occur as students participate in cocurricular activities became another divisional goal. In the initial phase of this project, self-reported measures of growth were collected from students. Preliminary findings have indicated that students are aware of, and report, skill development in communications, management, problem solving, organization, and citizenship. We have also found that the grade point averages of students who have participated in two or more organizations are significantly higher than the mean grade point average on campus (Carr and Zeller, 1988).

Cross-Cultural Residence Hall. The Office of Residence Life has developed a specialized housing facility for international and domestic students. In an effort to increase students' cross-cultural awareness and interaction skills, workshops will be presented throughout the year. A three-hour course entitled "Cross Cultural Communication" has been scheduled for students living in this residence hall. In addition, independent study opportunities will be offered to students wanting more intensive experiences.

Freshman Year Experiences. The university hopes to "front load" academic and student affairs resources toward the freshman year. The freshman seminar is a good example of the collaboration that is possible. The intention is to help new students adjust rapidly to the university, identify more closely with it, and experience greater satisfaction.

The following student affairs initiatives have been implemented: For the first time, a campus orientation for new freshmen was offered the weekend before the start of classes. A variety of activities were provided to help students adjust to college life and get to know each other and the campus. In addition, new freshmen have been housed in a common area to facilitate direct interactions with staff. Peer advisers have been added as staff members in the freshman housing area. These students serve as front-line academic advisers and will assist students with their academic adjustment to college life. In addition, student resource centers have been added to the residential areas. These offices provide convenient access to information and are staffed by peer advisers and other student affairs staff.

Faculty Involvement Outside the Classroom. Like their colleagues on many campuses, faculty at Southeast differ on the importance of cocurricular activities. When a campus-wide survey was conducted recently to assess faculty attitudes, the limited number of respondents supported the general goals and functions of student affairs. The survey stirred considerable dissonance, however, toward the division's use of institutional resources to address these functions. As a result of this survey, several ways to increase informal interaction between faculty and students outside of the classroom have been developed. For example, approximately fifteen faculty members have volunteered to serve as mentors to students living in residence halls and have been "adopted" by individual floors. The president of the university is one of these volunteers. Our discussions of cocurricular activities have led to increased interest and involvement among faculty in out-of-class activities.

Conclusion

The importance of building campus-wide community and assuring students, faculty, and student affairs professionals that they matter has been well established in previous chapters. Southeast Missouri State University's recent efforts to create curricular-cocurricular partnerships while engaged in a ten-year revision of curriculum represents one effort to increase involvement and strengthen community. We hope that focusing attention on nine broad-based objectives of liberal education in both in-class and out-of-class activities will produce significant and lasting contributions.

References

American Council on Education. *Student Personnel Point of View.* Washington, D.C.: American Council on Education, 1937.

Association of American Colleges. *Integrity in the College Curriculum: A Report to the Academic Community.* Washington, D.C.: Association of American Colleges, 1985.

Association of American Colleges. *A New Vitality in General Education.* Washington, D.C.: Association of American Colleges, 1988.

Astin, A. W. *Achieving Educational Excellence: A Critical Assessment of Priorities and Practices in Higher Education.* San Francisco: Jossey-Bass, 1985.

Berg, T. G. "Student Development and Liberal Arts Education." *National Association of Student Personnel Administrators Journal,* 1983, *21* (1), 10–16.

Bowen, H. R. *Investment in Learning: The Individual and Social Value of American Higher Education.* San Francisco: Jossey-Bass, 1977.

Boyer, E. L. *College: The Undergraduate Experience in America.* New York: Harper & Row, 1986.

Carr, P., and Zeller, W. "Student Involvement Survey." Unpublished manuscript, 1988.

Chandler, J. W. "President's Message." *Association of American Colleges (AAC) Liberal Education,* 1987, *73* (1), 1.

Chickering, A. W., and Gamson, Z. F. "Seven Principles for Good Practice in Undergraduate Education." *American Association for Higher Education Bulletin,* 1987, *39* (7), 3–7.

Creeden, J. E. "Student Affairs Biases as a Barrier to Collaboration: A Point of View." *NASPA Journal,* 1988, *26* (1), 60–63.

Cross, K. P. "Teaching for Learning." *American Association for Higher Education Bulletin,* 1987, *39* (8), 3–7.

Forrest, A. *Increasing Student Competence and Persistence: The Best Case for General Education.* Iowa City, Iowa: American College Testing (ACT) National Center for the Advancement of Educational Practices, 1982.

Kuh, G. D., Shedd, J. D., and Whitt, E. H. "Student Affairs and Liberal Education: Unrecognized (and Unappreciated) Common Law Partners." *Journal of College Student Personnel*, 1987, *28* (3), 252-259.

Miller, T. K., and Prince, J. S. *The Future of Student Affairs: A Guide to Student Development for Tomorrow's Higher Education.* San Francisco: Jossey-Bass, 1977.

Smith, D. G. "The Next Step Beyond Student Development: Becoming Partners Within Our Institutions." *National Association of Student Personnel Administrators Journal*, 1982, *19* (4), 53-62.

Study Group on the Conditions of Excellence in American Higher Education. *Involvement in Learning.* Washington, D.C.: National Institute of Education, 1984.

William Zeller is director of Residence Life and Housing at Washington State University.

John Hinni is dean of University Studies at Southeast Missouri State University, Cape Girardeau.

James Eison is director of the Center for Teaching and Learning at Southeast Missouri State University, Cape Girardeau.

Chief student affairs administrators are responsible for activity programs and must seek a balance between freedom and control that fits their campus.

Freedom and Control in Campus Activities: Who's in Charge?

Arthur Sandeen

Chief student affairs officers often find irony in the administration of campus activity programs. These activities are considered critical to student growth and development by student affairs professionals but are generally ignored, or viewed as inconsequential, by many faculty and other administrators. Typically, faculty and administrators only ask about campus activities when a student group has done something that gets publicity.

It is easy to become confused or cynical about such matters. On the one hand, the institution may pay little attention to what student groups are doing and claim no responsibility for them when something negative happens; on the other, it may gladly claim partnership with groups whose actions reflect positively on it.

The most difficult challenge for chief student affairs officers regarding campus activities is to find the appropriate balance between freedom for student groups and responsibility for the institution. Failure to understand this issue has resulted in the termination of more than one student affairs officer and has confused, frustrated, and angered student groups. An institution's catalogue may have intellectually sound statements about

D. C. Roberts (ed.). *Designing Campus Activities to Foster a Sense of Community.*
New Directions for Student Services, no. 48. San Francisco: Jossey-Bass, Winter 1989.

freedom of expression and association for its students, but if a volatile incident occurs, the student affairs officer is often faced with demands that are inconsistent with these statements. Such demands usually call for institutional control, not freedom for student groups.

The following examples illustrate the tension between freedom and control in the administration of campus activities:

1. A public university has a long tradition of freedom of expression. Student groups register with the institution and in return are permitted to use campus facilities. An undergraduate political group has invited the Grand Dragon of the Ku Klux Klan to speak in the auditorium. There is a tremendous outcry from students, faculty, external groups, and others, claiming that the university cannot allow this person to speak on campus.

2. A private college has supported a daily student newspaper for over fifty years by providing it with office space in the union and a faculty adviser. Moreover, campus activity funds, which come from tuition, finance the paper. Despite the faculty adviser's warning, the student editors intend to print information about the college president's personal investments, an exposure that would surely result in the president's termination.

3. A public university takes a "hands off" attitude toward its twenty-five fraternities, all located adjacent to the campus. Several members of one house get an underage female drunk and then sexually assault her. Arrests are made, but the major demand from inside and outside the institution is for the university to control the actions of the fraternity and immediately ban the organization.

4. A private college allows student organizations to register and makes no judgments about their political or religious views so long as state laws are not violated. A group of gay students registers as an organization, mainly to use union facilities for its social events. The president has been told by several board members that such a group cannot be tolerated at the college.

5. The governing board at a public university has granted the student government association authority to allocate almost $3 million per year to various student organizations and to intercollegiate athletics. The athletic allocation has been about a third of the total allocation for the past several years. When the institution is placed on probation by the National Collegiate Athletic Association for the illegal recruitment of athletes, the student government association becomes upset with the lack of integrity in athletics and decides to cancel funds for the program. Supporters of the athletic program demand that the institution compel the students to allocate the money. Student government refuses.

These are real situations, and most chief student affairs officers recognize them, as they have been expected to resolve similar situations for their institutions. Given the volatility of some incidents, conflicts regarding campus activities will always arise. There are many "stakeholders" in the process—students, faculty, the president, the governing board, various public groups, and the student affairs staff itself. Indeed, the success of the campus activities program at an institution may depend on how much congruence there is among these stakeholders about issues of freedom and control. The chief student affairs officer is responsible for informing these diverse groups about the purposes of the campus activities program and for achieving some agreement among them. Unless this is done, confusion, bitterness, and confrontation are inevitable.

In working with the various groups associated with campus activities, administrators should consider the following:

President

Most student affairs officers understand that the president's support is essential for the success of any general policy. If the president is ambivalent about the freedom-control issue or is inconsistent in decisions regarding activities, student affairs staff and students will likely be frustrated. Presidents should be reminded that it is in their own best interest to be clear and consistent. The chief student affairs officer cannot administer an activities program effectively without being confident of the president's philosophy and support. Whether the president has control or freedom as the top priority is not as important as clear and consistent application of policy. The student affairs staff cannot succeed if their own priorities are at odds with the president's. Furthermore, the chief officer should inform the president about the negative consequences of an inconsistent policy in the campus activities program. If there is significant disagreement, the student affairs staff will be faced with two unpleasant alternatives—administering a policy to which they are not committed or resigning.

In the earlier example of the gay student organization, the president should have had a clear understanding with the governing board about such matters before any such group appeared. Some presidents may prefer to avoid such conversations with their boards, but the confusion and anger that inevitably result from a lack of policy are far more damaging than the temporary unpleasantness of good planning. Chief student affairs officers must convince their presidents that this planning is necessary.

Not all institutions or presidents will take the same stance on the freedom-control issue in campus activities. Colleges and universities differ widely in their educational, social, and religious goals, and there will be corresponding differences in how their campus activities programs are conducted. Student affairs officers should serve the special missions of their institutions, and they should assist their presidents to be consistent with these missions as well.

Students

It is hazardous to write about students on an issue such as freedom and control in campus activities, because there is no orthodoxy in their thinking and no uniform point of view that accurately describes them. On any campus student views range from left to center to right on all issues with a considerable number not having any view at all. For the volatile situations cited earlier in this chapter, students would likely hold widely divergent opinions as to the best course of action for the institution.

If this diversity among students does not perplex administrators trying to construct a sensible activities policy, the "healthy rebelliousness" of many young people certainly makes the effort challenging. Institutional administrators often serve a useful function for young students as perfect targets for their political jibes and ambitions. More than one student body president has won a campus election by campaigning against "authoritarian, distant, and bureaucratic" administrators while privately joking about such tactics with those same administrators the day after the election. Some student leaders may spend a good deal of their time crusading for campus freedoms while fully recognizing that their own visibility and popularity depends on others believing these freedoms to be absent. Only the completely naive student affairs administrator would suggest that writing a "campus activities policy" will eliminate all conflict between students and the institution on the freedom-control issue. In fact the best student affairs administrators recognize that some conflict is not only inevitable but desirable if students are going to learn something.

Campus activity programs can provide pleasant recreation, but if that is all they do, the student affairs staff is cheating students out of a marvelous opportunity to learn about life. The goal of campus activities programs ought not to be a bland harmony but a lively and diverse debate about issues. Above all, institutions are obliged to be honest with their students. If a student government has no authority to act without the approval of the president, then it can hardly be called student government. If a fee allocation committee's decisions can be vetoed or changed by the president, members of the group should be so informed before they are appointed. If a student entertainment committee does not have the authority to invite anyone it wants to the campus, then it deserves to know what its limits are. If an institution's educational philosophy proscribes certain student groups on religious, sexual, or political grounds, the institution should state clearly and publicly why this is the case. If a college cannot permit the student newspaper to be editorially free, then it should not call it a student newspaper and should clearly state that the college itself is the editor and publisher.

Students deserve to know where they stand and what their role is within the institutional governance structure. Student affairs administrators should work with student leaders to formulate policy statements on issues as diverse as admissions, tuition, health, child care, student residences, athletics, academic policies, faculty evaluation, and selection of presidents. By involving students in these and many other campus issues, student affairs administrators can help students learn.

Despite any success in clarifying policy, student affairs administrators will always meet with some tension on the freedom-control issue. On the other hand, too cozy a relationship between the student political or editorial leader and the campus administrator may be intellectually or morally compromising for the student. For the administrator, such coziness may become almost parental at times, lacking the objectivity needed for good education.

The advantage of clear, written policy statements is that they give students and administrators a common starting place. The disadvantage is that they may mislead either group into thinking that written statements will cover all issues and problems. Moreover, students are by definition developing their values, ideas, and commitments while in college, yet not at the same pace or level. A written policy may address vital aspects of the student-institution relationship but is likely to be silent on the equally important matter of differences among individuals. For example, the student affairs staff works in a somewhat different manner with a group of senior law students planning a campus debate than it does with a group of freshmen planning a residence hall dance.

Faculty

The faculty are even more diverse in their views than the students. Since it is virtually impossible to get a consensus from the faculty about campus activities and since a large number of faculty do not seem interested anyway, why should student affairs staff concern themselves?

The faculty on any campus represent the greatest resource for a successful activities program. Without the participation of faculty, activities programs become separate appendages of the institution and are likely to be void of intellectual content. While it is true that the promotion-reward system does not encourage faculty to spend much time on campus activities, student affairs staff must actively encourage faculty participation and recognize it. If students rarely see faculty at events outside the classroom, they are likely to think that what they are doing has little importance or that no one of stature at their institution really cares. This compartmentalization of experience is common on campuses today and is the major reason student affairs staff want faculty to actively participate with students in improving the community life of the campus.

Student organizations are usually expected to have faculty advisers or sponsors. Faculty decide to volunteer their time as activities advisers because of their interest or expertise in a special area; they are rarely concerned about the freedom-control issue. Usually, however, situations arise that raise questions about the student-institution relationship. When this occurs, is the faculty adviser responsible for the actions of the student group? Is the adviser expected to enforce the college's rules and regulations, or is this someone else's responsibility? The chief student affairs administrator should write a clear policy statement defining the roles and responsibilities of faculty advisers. This should be done in conjunction with the major faculty group on campus and with the approval of the president. Major student organizations should thoroughly understand the policy so that their expectations for faculty advisers are clear.

With the increasing pressure on faculty to do research and publish, it is more difficult for student affairs staff to convince faculty to participate in student life. If faculty are unsure about their responsibilities to the institution in their role as advisers, it will be even more difficult to gain their support. Whatever the institutional policy is on the freedom-control issue, the chief student affairs officer must communicate it clearly to the faculty.

External Groups

Campus activities often become visible to outside groups because they frequently deal with volatile issues. Student affairs administrators may have to spend a considerable amount of time explaining or justifying institutional policies to external groups. Some groups, of course, will disagree with the institution regardless of the rationale, and every college has to live with such problems. However, if the institution has not taken time to formulate a clear position on its campus activities program, then it becomes vulnerable to criticism. The institution should be consistent in its stated public policy and in the application of that policy. External groups may not agree, but at least they will be aware of the college's position. The chief student affairs officer is responsible for informing these groups about the policy. The more this can be done before there are serious problems the more effective it will be. If the first contact with an external group is in the middle of a crisis, very little can be accomplished.

Student Affairs Staff

Student affairs staff are in general strongly committed to campus activities because these experiences can matter so much in the lives of students, both before and after their graduations. As a result they properly focus most of their efforts on the benefits students can receive rather than the content of the activity. Occasionally, inexperienced staff may identify so strongly with a particular issue that they lose their objectivity with student organizations, but in the great majority of cases this does not happen.

A formidable challenge to the chief student affairs administrator is to write a campus activities policy that can be adopted by the student affairs staff itself. There is great diversity in the purposes of student groups, and student affairs staff have very strong feelings themselves about the appropriate stance to adopt on the freedom-control issue. Long-term practices and strongly held convictions may have to be revised when legal restrictions are imposed, a new president is appointed, or a changed governing board takes over. Student affairs staff may be the most resistant to change of any group on campus because of their professional commitments. Despite the difficulty in formulating a consistent policy with the student affairs staff, the chief student affairs officer must achieve this goal. Failure to present a consistent policy will quickly be picked up by students and exploited. It will be unfair to student groups and confusing for faculty advisers and the public. Finally, it will surely result in difficulty for the institution and will likely lead to termination for the chief student affairs officer.

Policy Suggestions

In the process of formulating policy for campus activities, administrators should consider the following:
- The educational mission of the institution
- The priorities of the president
- The social and educational needs of the students
- Legal considerations pertinent to the institution
- The willingness of faculty to participate
- The support of the student affairs staff
- Student participation in establishing and revising the policy
- The establishment of a faculty-student policy council to review the policy and its application
- The needs (for example, concerts, child care, cooperative living groups) of special student groups.

Student affairs professionals spend only a small portion of their time worrying about the freedom-control issue in campus activities. Most of their efforts fortunately focus on the educational development of students. Nevertheless, the institution must be explicit and honest about the role of student leaders, and it must formulate and implement consistent policies regarding student leadership. Each college and university should develop its own policy reflecting its educational mission. Within this policy, student affairs staff must be sensitive to individual differences among students.

Arthur Sandeen is vice-president for student affairs and professor of educational leadership at the University of Florida. He is a past president of the National Association of Student Personnel Administrators and chaired the committee that authored A Perspective on Student Affairs *in commemoration of the 1937* Student Personnel Point of View.

Value education has become a very popular issue in higher education.

Value Education Through Activities Involvement

Dennis C. Roberts, Laura Brown

In the last decade value education has become extremely popular in higher education. Numerous national and global crises have demonstrated that educators must deal more aggressively with intellectual issues and must do so from the perspective of both scientific facts and subjective values.

This chapter will explore how value education can be related to the concern for community and mattering. Clearly value statements are made whether the activities planner intends to make them or not. In fact, what is not addressed in programming is sometimes more telling than what is deliberately said.

The key issues of this discussion will include (1) the origin of valuing and the methods used to convey a sense of valuing in our interactions with others, (2) examples of activities programs that overtly address values, and (3) a discussion of how previous chapters have led us to a point where the challenging pursuit of value education may be accomplished.

Origin of Valuing

The authors have attempted through this volume to establish the most important issues—and therefore the values—for their work in cam-

D. C. Roberts (ed.). *Designing Campus Activities to Foster a Sense of Community.*
New Directions for Student Services, no. 48. San Francisco: Jossey-Bass, Winter 1989.

pus activities. Like the bottom-line issues for individuals and organizations, the values inherent in building community through activities are fairly simple.

- Individuals are important to educational activities and are recognized and affirmed for their unique contributions
- Individuals should relate to one another to achieve both individual and group goals
- Organizations and educational environments are powerful and active sources for the individual's development
- Individuals are made to feel they matter when they are accorded attention, importance, ego-extension, dependence, and appreciation
- Attention to rituals and inclusiveness helps create an environment that conveys a sense of mattering
- Community is both the goal and outcome of concrete efforts in the above areas.

These values are similar to the original values espoused in *Student Personnel Point of View* (American Council on Education, 1937). They are merely restatements in terms of campus activities programs. Ideally, these values place activities programming in the mainstream of the educational setting and also serve to complement the other purposes and goals of the institution.

There are other complementary values than those espoused within our profession; they establish the importance of the ideas we have explored throughout this volume. Scott Peck's perspective on values provides an especially powerful model for understanding valuing in the context of activities and community building.

Peck is used for the primary view on valuing in this chapter because his unique and cogent discussion of *inclusiveness* is closely aligned with the ideas of mattering and community. In *The Different Drum: Community Making and Peace* (1987), he describes community as "not merely a matter of including different sexes, races, and creeds. It is also inclusive of the full range of human emotions. Tears are as welcome as laughter, fear as well as faith. And different lifestyles: hawks and doves, straights and gays, Grailers and Sears Roebuckers, the talkative and the silent. All 'soft' individuality is nurtured" (pp. 61-62).

As if to provide the definitive commentary on the importance of inclusiveness to community, he turns to its alternative. "The great enemy of community is exclusivity. Groups that exclude others because they are poor or doubters or divorced or sinners or of some different race or nationality are not communities; they are cliques—actually defensive bastions against community" (p. 61). If we support community development and accept the construct that thriving, viable, and sustaining communities must also be inclusive, then our challenge as student affairs professionals appears to be one of developing activities that will teach the value of inclusiveness. The primary objectives in working toward this goal are threefold: the integration of democratic decision making into student groups; the creation of an environment that supports appropriate risk taking for individual students and student groups; and the exploration of individual and group affirmation techniques for students and staff. We now turn to each of these objectives and their possible implications.

Democratic Decision Making. Quoting John R. Lucus, John Stott (1984) describes three steps for decision making:

> "The word 'democracy' and its derivatives apply to decision procedures," writes John R. Lucus in his book *Democracy and Participation.* It describes three aspects of the decision-making process. The first concerns who takes it. "A decision is democratically taken if the answer to the question 'who takes it?' is 'more or less everybody,' in contrast to decisions taken only by those best qualified to take them, as in a meritocracy." Secondly, democracy describes how a decision is reached. "A decision is taken democratically if it is reached by discussion, criticism, and compromise." Thirdly, democracy describes the spirit in which a decision is made, namely being concerned with the interests of all, instead of only a faction or a party [p. 92].

Democratic decision making in campus activities planning groups and student government groups represents in the broadest sense the principles of inclusiveness. Tasks for staff include training student leaders and participants in the arts of discussion, critical feedback, and appropriate compromise. In the selection of students for planning groups, recruits should represent all factions of a community and have the ability to comprehend the diversity of the campus population. Probably most important to the evaluation of decisions reached by a campus student group are the dynamics of the group itself. Staff must be available to process all activities and programs in relation to the entire campus community's response, not just the response of targeted groups.

Taking Risks. Students who are comfortable taking risks, which may only slightly deviate from traditional practice, understand something about individual differences. Even though they may not have an in-depth, theoretical knowledge base to support this understanding, they feel comfortable expressing their fears and frustrations, their hopes and dreams, their unpopular and popular ideas, and their unique strengths and weaknesses within their community.

Much has been written about college students in regard to understanding individual differences as a function of gender, age, ethnic and socioeconomic background, and so forth. Of particular interest to the campus activities planner may be an examination of individual learning styles and personality differences.

It is not uncommon for program planners, although providing a variety of topics, to become comfortable with the plan and format of a program or activity. Oftentimes the repetition of program formats that "have worked in the past" can overlook the need for a diversity of formats. The Learning Style Inventory, developed at Harvard University by David Kolb, can be a helpful planning tool for the development of campus programs (Kolb, 1984). The inventory is a brief forced-choice instrument in which subjects identify themselves as accommodators, divergers, assimilators, or convergers. These four categories correlate with the vocations people may desire, with their strengths and weaknesses, and with the ways they learn best. "Kolb's theory says that people learn through feeling (concrete experience, CE), watching (reflective observation, RO), thinking (abstract conceptualization, AC), and doing (active experimentation, AE)" (Stice, 1987, p. 105).

Another helpful tool for the campus activities programmer is the Myers-Briggs Type Indicator, which can be used as a predictor of patterns of student participation in activities (Provost and Anchors, 1987). As a personality inventory, it reveals the individual's preferences for making decisions, relating to the world, processing information, and in a word, living. Using this tool, a campus activities office can learn what types of activities appeal to different students and how to market programs either to specific populations or an entire campus community. As an example, while some students participate in structured, well-organized programs that offer them a chance to have an impact, other students join groups that offer unstructured, adventurous experiences (Provost and Anchors, 1987).

To the degree that campus activities recognize and celebrate the diversity of the community they are serving, the community, with all of its rich diversity, will respond. Attendance at programs and events will represent the entire community, and long-term involvement will become apparent. So-called majority groups will feel comfortable redefining exclusive program goals and formats to include minority or marginal groups without the expectation of conformity. In effect, the measure of the inclusiveness of activities is the extent to which the entire community—students and staff alike—is comfortable with risk taking.

Affirmation. Techniques of affirmation, demonstrated through activities programming in both the academic and cocurricular realm, provide the capstone to building community on any campus. Expressions of affirmation, when provided in an unconditional manner, seal the message of inclusion to all community members. Particular techniques of affirmation will differ depending on individual differences of persons and groups and the nature of the event or accomplishment to be recognized. Regardless of the final program plan, the activities planner must understand the relationship between affirmation and its inherent contribution to the support and stability of the students' self-concept. If in fact students are to feel affirmed and therefore valued within their community, activities must be designed to foster a sense of belonging and worth.

Belongingness, the awareness of being wanted, accepted, desired, or sought out by another person or group, is integral to each student's sense of inclusion within a community. When students leave home for the first time as traditional-age students or enter a campus as older, nontraditional-age students, the quest for a place "to fit" can take many forms. For some students, merely joining a student organization will support their need to belong; for others, having access to activities and programs that enhance their interests and allow for freedom of expression will be essential. Possibilities are endless. For the campus activities planner, providing special-interest organizations, minority-focused groups, and nonexclusive activities sponsored by majority groups will be critical.

As students experience a sense of belonging, they will also develop trust. This trust is placed not only in the belief that their uniqueness will be represented in their absence but that decisions reached by activities planners will encourage an attitude of worthiness in all community members. Worthiness, a feeling that "I count" and a sense of others endorsing our actions, is necessary for the risk-taking behavior that sometimes accompanies a student's first involvement in an activity. If campus activities are meant to promote inclusiveness and the development of community, then community members must have the confidence to participate. Activities planners can support students' self-esteem to the extent that all community members feel valued, worthy, and confident to participate. Examples of this support might include programs that recognize all religious holidays, student government groups that represent all academic majors, affirmative action practices that are built into selection processes for leadership positions, restructured social programs that allow as many activities for persons with few social skills as for those with many skills, and the celebration of academic transitions that move beyond convocation and graduation (Wagner, 1975).

Community Is Inclusiveness. Throughout the preceding discussion of community, inclusiveness, and activities programs, many terms that are not new to activities planners have been mentioned. A goal for the educational and social programs of most student affairs professionals is the development of community on their campuses. It may prove helpful for these professionals to reorient their focus to planning activity programs that actively teach the value of inclusiveness. If in fact we foster truly inclusive communities, then questions of governance, power, equal representation, and recognition of individuality may already be addressed.

Activities That Demonstrate Valuing

The preceding section has argued that specific values can inject substance and purpose into activities programs. Peck's (1987) perspective is easily adapted to the ultimate purpose of activities, which is to create educational programs that build a sense of community. To fulfill this purpose, professionals must do more than act on their personal values, they must be constantly alert for opportunities to teach values.

We now turn to other examples, which will demonstrate how values can be explored through specific activities. As mentioned in the introduction to this chapter, we convey our values as much by what we do not as by what we do include in the cocurriculum. Consider in each of the following examples what would happen or what the message would be if the approach were not used.

Convocations and Graduations. These ceremonial occasions are probably the most visible and long-standing examples of value education in higher education. There is always great pomp and ceremony at these important passages. But what lies beneath the pomp? Is the occasion really only a dusty relic that offends only history if abandoned? What inspiration and exploration of purpose lies behind the regalia, the music, and the ritual?

Convocations and graduations can be ideal opportunities for student affairs professionals and faculty to join together and identify issues of ultimate concern to the community. If ceremony is taken seriously, the following changes might be seen:

1. Instead of students being passive observers at the convocation procession, they are invited to join the faculty as a symbolic, intellectual journey.

2. The welcoming statements become more than obligatory gestures and instead include personal reflections and invitations from leaders of key constituents, including students, faculty, boards, and administration.

3. Students, faculty, and all others are invited to learn and repeat school mottoes, songs, and gestures. This is not done as a habit but is deliberately identified as a teaching opportunity, a time to draw the neophyte into the community.

4. Diversity of the community is demonstrated whenever possible. Males and females of all ages, races, and backgrounds should be visible.

5. Attempts are made to make everyone including newcomers feel comfortable rather than separated by a lack of knowledge of what is expected. Humor is a critical part of these events; everyone is relieved to reflect on the human predicament of new beginnings.

The topics of convocation and graduation speeches are also critical. Furthermore, what kind of message is sent when it appears that the major criterion for selecting speakers is their status and visibility? That great accomplishments can come from modest beginnings would be a worthy message to convey through the choice of a graduation speaker. Finally, are speeches simply waterfront pronouncements intended to offend no one, or are they intellectually challenging, do they push the community's boundaries of understanding?

In 1984 James Avery, chaplain of Northwestern University, spoke to graduating seniors about some of the ultimate concerns of life. In his baccalaureate address, "The Color Purple," he shared the scene from Alice Walker's *The Color Purple* (1982) where Celie cries out in anger:

> God gave me a lynched daddy, a crazy mama, a lowdown dog of a step pa, and a sister I probably won't ever see again. Anyhow, I say the God I been praying and writing to is a Man. And act just like all the other mens I know: Trifling, forgitful, and lowdown. . . . If He ever listened to poor colored women the world would be a different place, I can tell you—All my life I never care what people thought bout nothing I did, I say. But deep in my heart I cared about God. What He going to think. And come to find out, He don't think. Just sits up there glorying in being deef, I reckon [p. 164].

Celie's friend Shug then challenges her to look for God in common places. "God don't look like nothing. God ain't a picture show. God ain't something you can look at apart from anything else, including yourself. I believe God is everything. Everything that is or ever was or ever will be. And when you can feel that, and be happy to feel that, then you've found it. . . . God love everything you love—and a mess of stuff you don't. But more than anything else, God love admiration." Celie asks if God is then vain. Shug replies, "Naw, not vain. God just wants to share a good thing. I think it pisses God off if you walk by the color purple in a field somewhere and don't notice it" (p. 167).

The choice of quoting an uneducated black woman in an address to privileged, predominantly white students demonstrates that deep wisdom can be found among people of diverse stations in life. The content of the quote also draws attention to personal responsibility and the power we all have to create and find good in the world. The ritual of convocation and graduation can be enlivened to consider the ultimate values of life when we are allowed and encouraged to slow down, look beyond the ceremony, and learn.

Volunteerism and Community Service. Theus (1988) questions in her article "Campus-Based Community Service: New Populism or 'Smoke and Mirrors' " whether the apparent trend in the late 1980s toward volunteerism is real or not. She identifies a national trend led by college presidents and student leaders side by side that raises concern for the welfare of others to a new high. With only modest predictions of student service on 350 campuses—an average of 500 students each providing 4 hours of service per week—a phenomenal 21 million service hours per year are estimated. The monetary contribution of this service to others is estimated to exceed $105 millon (Theus, 1988).

That service to others is raised to such a level is a significant affirmation of values. On some campuses the value statement is so strong that students are almost perceived to be selfish and insensitive if they do not volunteer their time. Instead of volunteering being a drudgery obligation, it now ranks with going to the movies or a party with friends.

Leadership Programs. Leadership programs can clearly communicate the value of being involved with one's community. Leadership programs should be inclusive, that is, they should make all students feel welcome to participate. Most statements of institutional goals clearly establish the importance of preparing students for civic leadership and involvement in their communities. The leadership program can take advantage of this institutionally established priority by building support for a comprehensive program designed to reach a broad number of students and their organizations (Roberts, 1980).

In addition to inclusiveness and community service, leadership programs can exercise a deep concern of faculty—the application of concepts learned in the classroom to the habits and activities of students. A well-conceived and -implemented leadership program can accomplish tremendous strides in establishing collaborative opportunities with academic colleagues on the campus.

Off-Campus Residences. As enrollments swell for many campuses, deans of students have become embroiled in the issue of whether the college should monitor the behavior of students off campus. To many deans the response is a legal one. "The college is limited in its supervision of students to the campus proper—to attempt to extend intervention to other areas would invite the risk of liability for overseeing areas that are, practically, uncontrollable." To other deans the response is an educational one, "Students are legal adults and must be responsible for their own behavior. The college must deal with more important issues than attempting to modify the off-campus behavior of students."

An alternative approach to either of the above and one that conveys the value of community would be for the college to actively teach students their responsibilities as adults in a neighborhood community. The satisfaction of the needs and concerns of community members must be negotiated to serve the largest number. Residence halls are early opportunities for younger students to learn, under closer supervision, to live in community. Only students who master the skill of living in community are allowed to move into the broader community to enjoy their full adult responsibilities as neighborhood members. The dean's office becomes a resource for teaching and coaching students in establishing positive relationships with neighbors. This approach sends a clear message that creating community is a shared responsibility of students, faculty, and administrators alike.

Alcohol and Other Drug Abuse Prevention. This is undoubtedly one of the most difficult areas of student affairs in which to make value statements that do not alienate students from the institution. With trends toward continued alcohol use by underage students, the creation, statement, and enforcement of policy that is consistent with law almost guarantees a student-administration standoff. Yet the law must be respected if we are to be ethical.

Another approach, taken by Pavela (1988) in new-student orientation briefings at the University of Maryland, is to ask the students to visualize a retirement banquet. He tells them the banquet is for a person who has contributed greatly to both the work setting and the broader community. "Now," he says, "the person is you." He then directs students to write down things they would hope to hear at such a retirement banquet. Students list statements related to loyalty, energy, contribution, creativity, and honesty. Pavela goes on, "Now let me tell you what you didn't say. You didn't say that Mary wore the best clothes of anyone on campus. Joe could drink anybody under the table. You didn't say that driving the fastest and raciest car on campus was important to success." The purpose of this exercise is to encourage students to look at ultimate values, not simply the transient values prevalent in many undergraduate environments—like partying, conforming, and looking good.

Taking an ultimate stance on alcohol and other drug abuse, like the one described above, moves the student-administration conflict over prohibition into a new arena. In this new arena students consider what they ultimately want to achieve and how their current behavior relates to those goals. We also acknowledge the importance of such an issue to the campus community as a whole.

We have explored in some depth how values are addressed both through our daily interactions and through more strategically designed programs, that is, through new approaches to old problems. Clearly mattering and community are values in and of themselves. Furthermore, the choice to address a particular issue or behave in a specific way is a value statement; not making these choices makes just as strong a statement. We must maintain a focus on values in all our actions so that statements are not made by default or important questions left unexplored.

Conclusion

This book begins with a foreword by Esther Lloyd-Jones, one of the original and probably the most instrumental drafters of the philosophical statement that brought student personnel work into being. Community is clearly one of the most visible and critical values underpinning that work. The drafters of *Student Personnel Point of View* (American Council on Education, 1937) urged those in student personnel to view each student as a unique individual and, further, to look at how community building affects the education and development of the individual. Communities thereby become powerful sources for the development of all their members.

From 1937 to the present, we in higher education have pursued numerous initiatives to enliven campuses as educational and developmental settings. During this period, the intention to look at and shape communities has been more or less visible. This volume has attempted to renew interest in the concept of community. By focusing on community, the campus activities planner can more purposefully design and deliver programs and, more importantly, relate these programs to the mission of the institution.

Several propositions are essential in understanding the relationship of the individual to the community and the importance of community to the higher education institution. Schlossberg helped us understand how individuals relate to communities through her discussion of mattering and marginality. Communities are created when individual students, faculty, and staff believe that they are part of and that they matter to their college or university. The challenge is to send clear messages of mattering to these persons. To that end the authors of this volume have offered the following insights on building community. We conclude with this summary of main points:

1. A sense of mattering is felt when we are given attention; our presence and perspectives are seen as having importance; our successes and failures are in some way felt by those around us; we are interconnected by our dependence on one another; and we are appreciated by others, as demonstrated through their gestures.

2. A community that conveys a sense of mattering to its members pays attention to rituals.

3. A community that embraces differences among its members celebrates community and individuality at the same time.

4. The assessment of community attributes is critical to positive change. When designed and used properly, assessment becomes part of the process of creating community.

5. A sense of community depends on the purposeful coordination of campus programs and services.

6. Faculty and staff are essential to the creation of community as is the elimination of barriers among campus constituencies.

7. Decision making, priority setting, and change are a natural part of any active community. Clear expectations about roles and governance help avoid circumstances that can undermine community.

8. Value education can be both the goal and process of creating a community. Values can be actively explored through campus activities programs. Inclusiveness and involvement clearly demonstrate the values of any organization.

9. Mattering and community are crucial to student satisfaction, retention, success, and loyalty for the learning environment.

References

American Council on Education. *Student Personnel Point of View.* Washington, D.C.: American Council on Education, 1937.

Avery, J. E. "The Color Purple." Baccalaureate address at Northwestern University, June 15, 1984.

Kolb, D. A. *Experiential Learning: Experience as the Source of Learning and Development.* Englewood Cliffs, N.J.: Prentice-Hall, 1984.

Pavela, G. "Legal Issues." Keynote address for National Collegiate Drug Awareness Week Kick-Off Conference, Washington, D.C., February 11, 1988.

Peck, M. S. *The Different Drum: Community Making and Peace.* New York: Simon & Schuster, 1987.

Provost, J. A., and Anchors, S. "Student Involvement and Activities." In J. Provost and S. Anchors (eds.), *Applications of Meyers-Briggs Type Indicators in Higher Education.* Palo Alto, Calif.: Consulting Psychologists Press, 1987.

Roberts, D. C. (ed.). *Student Leadership Programs in Higher Education.* Alexandria, Va.: American College Personnel Association, 1980.

Stice, J. E. "Further Reflections: Useful Resources." In J. E. Stice (ed.), *Developing Critical Thinking and Problem-Solving Abilities.* San Francisco: Jossey-Bass, 1987.

Stott, J. *Involvement: Being a Responsible Christian in a Non-Christian Society.* Old Tappan, N.J.: Fleming H. Revell, 1984.

Theus, K. T. "Campus-Based Community Service: New Populism or 'Smoke and Mirrors.'" *Change,* Sept./Oct. 1988, pp. 27–38.

Wagner, M. E. *The Sensation of Being Somebody.* Grand Rapids, Mich.: Zondervan Publishing House, 1975.

Walker, A. *The Color Purple.* New York: Harcourt Brace Jovanovich, 1982.

Dennis C. Roberts is dean of student affairs at Lynchburg College, Lynchburg, Virginia, and has served as president of the American College Personnel Association. He writes on leadership programs, substance abuse, and student development.

Laura Brown is director of residence life at Southern Methodist University. She trains professionals and student leaders in counseling, programming, and community development.

*Deliberately involving students in campus activities through
an active participation game helps students address the
transition from marginality to mattering.*

Moving Through
Campus Activities

Roger W. Sorochty

Most readers would probably agree that their campuses do not offer activities as a means of filling up students' idle time. Rather, most would probably concur with comments made by Esther Lloyd-Jones in the foreword and originally espoused in *Student Personnel Point of View* (American Council on Education, 1937). All activities—those in class as well as those out of class—should be viewed as having the potential to influence the development and education of students.

This appendix describes Kansas Newman College's "Discover Newman" game, which deliberately involves students in campus activities using the format of an active, participatory game based on the notion of wellness. The idea for this approach came from Murray and Apilado (1987). By using a variety of inducements to involve students in activities, the program eases students through the transition from feeling marginal to mattering.

Involvement, Success, and Retention

As Schlossberg pointed out in Chapter One, Astin (1984) believes that students' satisfaction with college, academic achievement, and retention are directly correlated to their degree of involvement in the institution.

D. C. Roberts (ed.). *Designing Campus Activities to Foster a Sense of Community.*
New Directions for Student Services, no. 48. San Francisco: Jossey-Bass, Winter 1989.

By being involved in an institution, individuals feel a part of what is happening and a sense of community develops. The challenge for student affairs professionals is to provide as many opportunities as possible for students to become involved.

Students go through a variety of transitions and will feel marginal to some degree during these times. One of the most significant transitions is when the student first enters the institution. In addition, the highest rate of student attrition occurs prior to the sophomore year. Therefore, if we view attrition as a result of the student not feeling successful or not having a sense of well-being and we agree with Astin that involvement can enhance success, then clearly we should get students involved as soon as possible. The next section describes a program that addresses the student's first major transition—becoming involved in a new institution.

The First Transition

Promoting involvement in an array of campus activities places students in contact with a variety of services and offices as well as faculty, staff, and each other. As a result, they feel more familiar and comfortable with the institution, hence, less marginal. The format of a game makes the process more interesting to the student.

The "Discover Newman" Game. In the game "Discover Newman" the targeted activities and areas focus on the dimensions of wellness (Leafgren and Elsenrath, 1986). These dimensions encompass the areas of development in which students will be engaged and are thus an appropriate framework to use.

For the actual game, the target group for participation was incoming freshmen because of the nature of their transitional experience. However, because of the small size of our campus, all students could participate. Furthermore, all new freshmen are required to participate in an extended orientation course during the fall semester, entitled "Introduction to the Liberal Arts." The game is one of the components of the course.

Of course, the college cannot simply ask or require students to participate in something and call it a game. The real "hook" then became a raffle at the end of the game with degree of participation in the game determining how many raffle entries students received.

We wanted the game's theme to convey the idea of *moving through* a transition with all the excitement and unexpected occurrences such a journey implied. We also wanted to show students how they could make this journey. In the student handbook for the College at New Paltz (Student Life Staff, 1987) the college experience was described as an educational vehicle. The handbook was written in the style of an owner's manual, explaining how to operate this new vehicle successfully. From this idea we referred to the game as "The Discover Newman Road Rally," it being the first opportunity to road test the student's educational vehicle. The six wellness areas to be addressed by the game are shown on the cover of the booklet, as follows:

1. Physical health
2. Intellectual achievement
3. Social development
4. Spiritual growth
5. Career success
6. Emotional development.

Game booklets were distributed during fall registration and given to freshmen at the first meeting of the "Introduction to the Liberal Arts" class. The booklet first indicated areas students might get involved in during the "road rally." For example, they were told that they could "drive" toward spiritual growth, "accelerate" to career success, and "keep control" of emotional development.

Programs and activities were planned to take place at various times from the first day of the fall semester through October 31. Students had to get one token (in the shape of a spare tire for their educational vehicle) from each of the six wellness categories to qualify for one entry in the raffle, which was to be held at the end of the game. They could do this three times, for a total of eighteen different activities, to get three entries in the raffle. In addition, there were three other ways to get more entries into the raffle.

First, we believed that students would discover a great deal about the college if they attended summer orientation. Therefore, if they attended, they automatically received an entry in the raffle.

A crossword puzzle was also developed to help students learn about the institution. This was published in the college newspaper during the fourth week of the semester. A completely correct puzzle was worth another entry in the raffle.

Finally, a checklist for "what to do and who to see to get things done" was developed. The student had to match statements such as, "You've lost your I.D. card. To get it replaced, go to _____ ," with the appropriate person or office. If this list of thirty items was completed correctly, the student got another entry in the raffle. This option was especially designed for commuter and nontraditional students, who were not on campus as much as resident students and who therefore might not have been able to take advantage of the scheduled activities as easily.

The prizes in the raffle were selected for being of interest to students, thereby encouraging participation in the game. They included a Colorado ski trip, tickets to a Kansas City Chiefs game, and gift certificates for clothing, meals, video rentals, records, and so on. All were donated through requests made by staff and students of local merchants.

It is often difficult for students to see the long-term value of participating in out-of-class activities. Often this is not due to a lack of interest but simply the other demands on their time. This is especially true of commuter and nontraditional students, whose involvement on campus is more difficult to achieve than resident students'. Therefore, it was felt that students ought to see immediate, tangible rewards for their involvement. They were not inundated with the theoretical underpinnings of the game. The important point is that it worked; students did get involved.

Other Transitions

Students should have a clear idea of the purpose of a campus activities program. Most campuses require an organization to have a constitution or bylaws and an adviser. This defines the organization's purpose and helps prospective members decide if they want to join. Many campuses also encourage student organizations to participate in a "club fair," where students can find out about organizations and, again, decide which ones they want to join.

Student organizations must set and maintain goals for themselves as well as the individual members. The phrase, People support what they help create, was never more appropriate; it encompasses the concepts of involvement, success, mattering, and community. Constitutions and bylaws can do that to a certain extent. However, nothing takes the place of well-run meetings in guiding the organization and signaling its own transitions.

Closely related to an organization's success is the performance of student leaders. Here, students are certainly confronted with transitions and feelings of marginality and mattering. How, for example, does a student decide when to move from merely being a member to being a leader? And once such a transition is made, what can be done to maximize that student's chances for success? A more difficult transition results when the student runs for office but does not make it. Failure to address these issues increases the chance that a new student leader will not feel successful, which in turn may discourage future involvement in the same or other organizations, even beyond college.

Besides the transition from member to leader, another crucial transition occurs when the student must decide whether to pursue interests in other organizations or activities. This can be especially troublesome for the student if the transition means moving from leadership in one organization to just membership in another. The student must assess, possibly with help, the impact such a change would have on self-concept, feelings of worth, and so on.

Many professionals have probably seen students confront this problem. It may be more prevalent on smaller campuses, where a smaller number of students tend to be the ones involved in most of the organizations. Most staff could probably cite examples of students who moved from being members of clubs to becoming officers, members of other clubs or student government, and then student government officers. These moves entail transitions and potential feelings of marginality and mattering. Yet if properly prepared, students can negotiate these transitions successfully, increase their sense of involvement and success, and foster a sense of community, all resulting in their persistence with the institution.

The relationship of involvement to success, satisfaction, feelings of community, and retention has been demonstrated. But how do we get students to accept it? How do we help students achieve their own balance between cocurricular participation and academic performance? It is not that students are unconcerned about what happens to them or uninterested in getting the most for their educational dollar; they are simply exposed to competing demands for their time. Work, for example, is an increasingly important demand since it is often the only way to make college affordable.

Conclusion

Because the "Discover Newman" program just began, longitudinal data on retention or other program outcomes are unavailable. The hope, however, is that the game will substantiate the link between student involvement and feelings of success, well-being, and mattering with the related outcome of increased retention.

Preliminary anecdotal data are encouraging. Virtually every new freshman participated in the game. Even returning students took part, which because of the small size of our campus, was easy to accommodate. Colleagues in the state have asked for and received information about the game for consideration on their campuses. Most importantly, the game will be more prominent in Kansas Newman's extended freshman orientation class, "Introduction to the Liberal Arts." The faculty teaching the two-credit hour class will require every new student to participate in the game by attending at least one of each of the six types of activities.

A relationship does exist between student involvement on campus and wellness. It was first addressed in *Student Personnel Point of View* (American Council on Education, 1937), which recognized that a student's well-being is influenced by out-of-class experiences that contribute to the overall educational experience. Writings addressing the notion of wellness carried this belief one step further. Astin (1984) has attempted to show a correlation between involvement on campus and satisfaction with college as exhibited by students' academic achievement and retention. Therefore, the efforts we make in the area of student involvement are firmly grounded in our profession's founding document and reinforced

86

through more recent writings such as those on wellness, student development, and involvement and on the profession itself, like *A Perspective on Student Affairs* (Sandeen and others, 1987).

References

American Council on Education. *Student Personnel Point of View.* Washington, D.C.: American Council on Education, 1937.
Astin, A. W. "Student Involvement: A Developmental Theory for Higher Education." *Journal of College Student Personnel,* 1984, *24,* 297–308.
Leafgren, F., and Elsenrath, D. E. "The Role of Campus Recreation Programs in Institutions of Higher Education." In F. Leafgren (ed.), *Developing Campus Recreation and Wellness Programs.* New Directions for Student Services, no. 34. San Francisco: Jossey-Bass, 1986.
Murray, J., and Apilado, M. "Developing a Wellness-Based Orientation Program for Small Colleges." Paper presented at the American College Personnel Association/National Association of Student Personnel Administrators Convention, Chicago, 1987.
Sandeen, A., and others. *A Perspective on Student Affairs: A Statement Issued on the 50th Anniversary of the "Student Personnel Point of View."* Washington, D.C.: National Association of Student Personnel Administrators, 1987.
Student Life Staff. *The College at New Paltz Educational Vehicle: Owner's Manual for Service and Repair.* New Paltz, N.Y.: The College at New Paltz, 1987.

Roger W. Sorochty is vice-president for student affairs at Kansas Newman College, Wichita.

APPENDIX:
Other Resources

Astin, A. W. "Student Involvement: A Developmental Theory for Higher Education." *Journal of College Student Personnel*, 1984, *24*, 297–308.
    The author presents a theory of student development based on the concept of student involvement. Presenting other theories first, he then discusses the notion of students' time as a resource.

Astin, A. W. *Achieving Educational Excellence: A Critical Assessment of Priorities and Practices in Higher Education.* San Francisco: Jossey-Bass, 1985.
    Traditional assumptions about excellence often work against educational values and priorities. The author argues that involvement is the key to learning, and he provides strategies for increasing student involvement through changes, instructional methods, campus activities, and assessment procedures.

Astin, A. W. "Involvement: The Cornerstone of Excellence." *Change*, 1985, *17*, 35–39.
    This article challenges the trend of using reputation and resources as the main criteria for determining institutional excellence in higher education. The key to an effective learning experience is student involvement, that is, active participation in one's education both in and out of the classroom.

Barr, M. J., and Keating, L. A. (eds.). *Establishing Effective Programs.* New Directions for Student Services, no. 7. San Francisco: Jossey-Bass, 1979.
    The authors of this sourcebook focus on the implementation of new ideas as well as the maintenance of existing programs and present useful discussions of resource utilization, cross-departmental interaction, and staff development.

Berg, T. G. "Student Development and Liberal Arts Education." *National Association of Student Personnel Administrators Journal*, 1983, *21*, 10–16.
    This article presents a good case for the argument that liberal arts education and student development theory share a similar conceptual background. To educate liberally, learning experiences must facilitate growth of the whole person as well as promote intellectual maturity.

Boyer, E. L. *College: The Undergraduate Experience in America.* New York: Harper & Row, 1986.
    This text takes a poignant look at undergraduate education in the United States today and makes general recommendations for improving the quality of higher education. It focuses on the college experience from admissions through graduation and provides strategies for enhancing learning both in and out of the classroom. The author encourages campus constituents to work together to develop a community of learning in which all aspects of college life have a common sense of purpose.

Canon, H., and Brown, R. (eds.). *Applied Ethics in Student Services.* New Directions in Student Services, no. 30. San Francisco: Jossey-Bass, 1985.
    This sourcebook will help readers interested in the freedom-control issue in campus activities. It reviews the various ethical codes published by student affairs organizations and presents examples of problems and conflicts that demonstrate institutional and professional responsibilities.

Carlson, J. M., and Basler, M. "The Quiet Revolution: Student Activities and the Nontraditional Student." *Campus Activities Programming*, 1986, *19* (6), 52–56.
The authors identify the nontraditional student in reference to programming and look at programming ideas for minorities, women, and returning students.

Delworth, U., Hanson, G., and Associates. *Student Services: A Handbook for the Profession*. San Francisco: Jossey-Bass, 1985.
This comprehensive book provides a valuable background for the reader interested in the field of student affairs. Chapters Six to Nine are especially helpful in presenting different models for practice.

Forrest, A. *Increasing Student Competence and Persistence: The Best Case for General Education*. Iowa City, Iowa: American College Testing National Center for the Advancement of Educational Practices, 1982.
This report strongly advises institutions to view general education programs as being composed of both in-class and out-of-class experiences. "How courses are taught, the kind of advice students receive about the courses and what happens to students outside of the classroom are important factors in assisting or inhibiting student achievement of the intended outcomes of general education."

Garland, P. H. *Serving More Than Students: A Critical Need for College Student Personnel Services*. ASHE-ERIC Higher Education Report, no. 7. Washington, D.C.: Association for the Study of Higher Education, 1985.
The author discusses the role student affairs must play in higher education institutions as those institutions respond to changes in society. As student affairs works to enhance developmental possibilities for students, improve the quality of student life, and integrate students into the life of the campus, it adopts strategies that may be vital to the entire institution.

Kelly, J. G., and Hess, R. E. *The Ecology of Prevention: Illustrating Mental Health Consultation*. New York: Haworth Press, 1987.
Consultation is defined in this book as an ecological enterprise. Consultees are viewed as participants and key actors in the consultee organization, where the participants create resources for social support and self-direction.

Kuh, G. D. (ed.). *Evaluation in Student Affairs*. Washington, D.C.: American College Personnel Association, 1979.
This volume treats the general issues for evaluation in student affairs as well as specific issues for student affairs departments. It includes an effective guide for implementing evaluations and case studies for assisting the practitioner.

Kuh, G. D., Shedd, J. D., and Whitt, E. H. "Student Affairs and Liberal Education: Unrecognized (and Unappreciated) Common Law Partners." *Journal of College Student Personnel*, 1987, *28* (3), 252–259.
Since student affairs continues to assume tasks that faculty once performed in their role as educators, the dilemma remains how to reinstate the functions of student affairs into the academic mainstream. The authors urge student affairs professionals to collaborate more with like-minded faculty members to create environments that are conducive to learning both in and out of the classroom.

Leafgren, F. (ed.). *Developing Campus Recreation and Wellness Programs*. New Directions for Student Services, no. 34. San Francisco: Jossey-Bass, 1986.

This sourcebook is for those who want to build a campus activities and wellness program. The chapters range from the role of recreation and student housing programs to programs designed for the small college.

Manning, K. "The Multi-Cultural Challenge of the 1990s." *Campus Activities Programming*, 1988, *21* (3), 53–56.
This article presents a model for how student groups develop in their view of multi-culturalism. It provides guidelines to ensure that programs meet multicultural goals.

Miller, T. K., and Prince, J. S. *The Future of Student Affairs: A Guide to Student Development for Tomorrow's Higher Education.* San Francisco: Jossey-Bass, 1976.
This book explains the theory of student development. It evolved out of the Tomorrow's Higher Education project established in 1968 by the American College Personnel Association. It is the companion piece to, and follows, Robert Brown's *Student Development in Tomorrow's Higher Education: A Return to the Academy.*

Miser, K. M. *Student Affairs and Campus Dissent.* Washington, D.C.: National Association of Student Personnel Administrators, 1988.
This monograph includes historical analyses, current strategies, and institutional philosophies regarding dissent. It samples campus policies and presents some case studies.

Porter, J., Rosenfield, E., and Spaull, E. "Tapping Diversity Within Higher Education: Some Lessons Learned." *Association for Handicapped Student Service Programs in Post-Secondary Education Bulletin*, 1985, *3*, 79–86.
The authors look at the mainstreaming of disabled students and apply the concepts to all people. Diversity is viewed in terms of how institutions should foster interaction.

Sandeen, A., and others. *A Perspective on Student Affairs: A Statement Issued on the 50th Anniversary of the "Student Personnel Point of View."* Washington, D.C.: National Association of Student Personnel Administrators, 1987.
As the title indicates, this document sets forth the assumptions and purposes that underlie student affairs work after re-examining *Student Personnel Point of View.* The booklet gives a historical overview of the profession, describes the current context of higher education and a set of assumptions and beliefs that guide the work of student affairs, and concludes with a description of the role of student affairs today.

Smith, D. G. "The Next Step Beyond Student Development: Becoming Partners Within Our Institutions." *National Association of Student Personnel Administrators Journal*, 1982, *19* (4), 53–62.
Student development theory has been a major foundation for cocurricular program models by student affairs professionals. The author argues that student affairs professionals have a primary responsibility for serving the educational objectives of the institution and that student development models may create further dissonance and misunderstanding between student affairs and academic affairs.

Stewart, G. M., and Hartt, J. A. "Promoting a Multicultural Environment Through College Activities, Services, and Programs." *Boston 1987: Our Town Meeting.* Bloomington, Ind.: Association of College Unions-International, 1987.

This presents a model for promoting a multicultural environment. It includes the OASES program: Orientation, Affiliation, Support, Extension, Systemization.

Trickett, E. J., Kelly, J. G., and Vincent, T. A. "The Spirit of Ecological Inquiry in Community Research." In E. C. Susskind and D. C. Klein (eds.), *Community Research: Methods, Paradigms, and Applications.* New York: Praeger Press, 1985.

The authors present and discuss ten principles for carrying out community research.

Winston, R. B., Bonney, W. C., Miller, T. K., and Dagley, J. C. *Promoting Student Development Through Intentionally Structured Groups: Principles, Techniques, and Applications.* San Francisco: Jossey-Bass, 1988.

This volume is devoted to the use of student groups in advancing individuals toward their educational and developmental goals. It is geared toward the practical considerations of structured groups in the collegiate environment.

Index

A

Academic affairs, and student affairs, 49-58

Activities, campus. *See* Campus activities

Activities center, 45-47; staff of, 46. *See also* Campus activities

Adaptation, 21-22

Administration, of campus activities, 61-67

Affirmation, 72-73

Alcohol abuse, 21; prevention of, 77; research on, 23-24

Allen, W. R., 28, 36

American Council on Education, 1, 17, 25, 50, 58, 70, 77, 79, 81, 85

Anchors, S., 72, 79

Apilado, M., 81, 85

Appreciation, 10-11

Association of American Colleges, 50, 51, 58

Astin, A., 5, 14, 15, 28, 34, 36, 42, 45, 47, 49, 50, 51, 58, 81, 85, 87

Attention, 9-10

Austin, N., 41, 47

Avery, J. E., 75, 79

Ayala, F., 42, 47

B

Banning, J. H., 18, 25

Barr, M. J., 87

Basler, M., 28, 33, 37, 88

Batchelor, S., 43

Beck, E. T., 8, 15

Berg, T. G., 51, 58, 87

Berkowitz, A. D., 21, 25

Bernard, J., 28, 37

Bonney, W. C., 91

Bowen, H. R., 50, 58

Boyer, E. L., 27, 34, 36, 37, 49, 50, 58, 88

Bradford, L., 8

Brooks, G. C., Jr., 29, 37

Brown, L., 69, 79

Brown, R., 88

C

Calendaring, 45-46; at Southeast Missouri State University, 56

Campus activities, 39-40; administration of, 40-41, 61-67; coordination design for, 43-44; and ecological paradigm, 17-25; policy suggestions for, 67; rationale for coordinating, 41-43; student coordination of, 44-45. *See also* Activities center

Campus activities staff, and ecological paradigm, 18-25

Canon, H., 88

Carlson, J., 27, 28, 33, 37, 88

Carr, P., 57, 58

Chandler, J. W., 51, 58

Chavez, E., 27, 37

Chickering, A. W., 14, 15, 45, 47, 50, 51, 58

Clack, R. J., 18, 25

Community: as inclusiveness, 70, 73; and student personnel work, 1-3; as value, 70, 77-79

Commuter students, 34

Convocations, 74-75

Conyne, R. D., 18, 25

Coping, 21-22

Council for the Advancement of Experiential Learning, 11

Creeden, J. E., 53, 58

Cross, K. P., 51, 58

D

Dagley, J. C., 91

Dawson, M. E., 28, 37

DeCarbo, E., 35, 37

Delworth, U., 88

Dependence, 10

Disabled students, 34

"Discover Newman" game, 81-85

Diversity, of students, 28-29, 36, 90. *See also* Students

Dodder, R. A., 21, 25

Drug abuse: prevention of, 77; research on, 23-24